UNLOCKING THE STRENGTH OF VULNERABILITY: TO CONQUER NARCISSISM

Author

JOHN W. WILLIAMS JR.

THE HOLY BIBLE, NEW INTERNATIONAL VERSION®, NIV® Copyright © 1973, 1978, 1984, 2011 by Biblica, Inc.™ Used by permission. All rights reserved worldwide.

Copyright © 2023 John W. Williams Jr Ministries.

I wrote this book about Narcissism from a Christian perspective to help the victims of narcissism and the narcissist experience restoration and healing. I pray that the Lord will use it and in some small way, it will make a profound difference in the lives of the readers. I would like to thank my Family, Friends, and the wonderful Victims and the Narcissists who shared their stories.

- John W. Williams Jr., RN B.TH

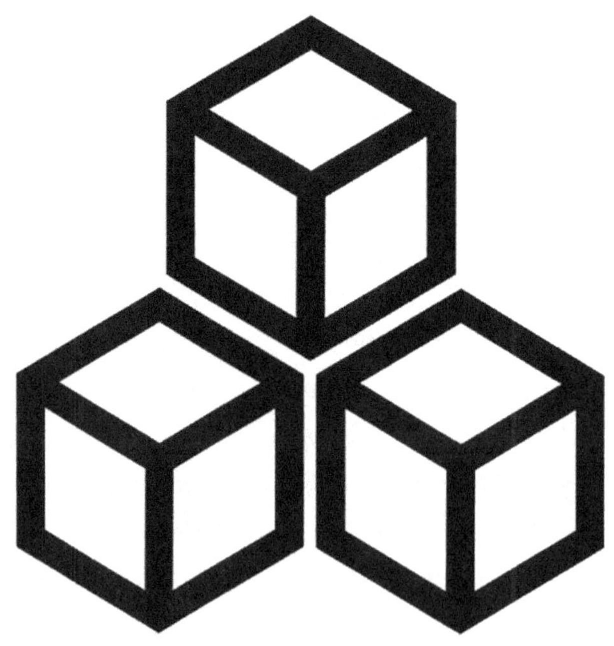

CONTENTS

INTRODUCTION

Narcissism, derived from the Greek myth of Narcissus, refers to excessive self-love and admiration. In contemporary society, it has become increasingly important to establish the prevalence of narcissism, particularly when considering the influence of media and the values it promotes. One starting point to understand the prevalence of narcissism is found in the Hollywood industry, which often presents stories revolving around self-centered characters. These narratives tend to celebrate and perpetuate a culture of self-obsession and self-validation. Moreover, society has witnessed a rise in self-centered and loveless behaviors, exemplified by individuals prioritizing their own needs and desires without considering the impact on others. These examples of Hollywood narcissistic stories and people being self-centered are indicative of a broader cultural shift that underscores the need to assess and address the prevalence of narcissism in today's society.

Proverbs 16:18 (NIV): "Pride goes before destruction, a haughty spirit before a fall."

Hollywood, with its glamorous portrayal of fame and success, often presents narcissistic narratives as enticing stories. These stories revolve around characters who prioritize their own needs above all else, seeking validation from external sources. Whether it is the self-aggrandizing persona of a famous actor or the obsession with physical appearance, these narratives present a distorted reflection of reality. By prominently featuring narcissistic characters in film and television, the industry contributes to the permeation of narcissism throughout society, ultimately shaping societal values and behaviors.

Philippians 2:3-4 (NIV): "Do nothing out of selfish ambition or vain conceit. Rather, in humility, value others above yourselves, not looking to your own interests but each of you to the interests of the others."

Society has witnessed a rise in self-centered behaviors where individuals place their own interests above everything else. The emphasis on personal success and instant gratification has led people to disregard the needs and feelings of those around them. Social media platforms amplify this phenomenon, where individuals often curate their digital presence to portray an idealized self-image. The constant need for validation and self-promotion further perpetuates narcissistic tendencies and fosters a culture of self-absorption.

Galatians 5:22-23 (NIV): "But the fruit of the Spirit is love, joy, peace, forbearance, kindness, goodness, faithfulness, gentleness, and self-control. Against such things, there is no law."

The erosion of genuine connections and the decline of empathy have become synonymous with the prevalence of narcissism. In a loveless society, individuals prioritize their own desires and experiences, neglecting the emotional well-being of others. As genuine connections are replaced by superficial interactions, such as online communication and virtual relationships, the ability to empathize and understand the feelings of others diminishes. This lack of empathy further contributes to the prevalence of narcissism, as self-interest takes precedence over building meaningful connections.

1 Peter 3:8 (NIV): "Finally, all of you, be like-minded, be sympathetic, love one another, be compassionate and humble."

It is crucial to assess and address the prevalence of narcissism in today's society to foster healthier relationships and promote empathy as a core value. Recognizing the influence of Hollywood's narcissistic storytelling and holding the media accountable for its role in shaping societal values is a starting point. Moreover, promoting self-awareness and emotional intelligence at an individual level can help combat the rise of self-centered behaviors. By encouraging genuine connections and fostering an environment of empathy, society can work towards dismantling the prevalence of narcissism and embracing a more compassionate and supportive culture. Only through collective efforts to counter narcissistic tendencies can we cultivate a society that values meaningful relationships and prioritizes the well-being of others.

Ephesians 4:32 (NIV): "Be kind and compassionate to one another, forgiving each other, just as in Christ God forgave you."

This is not something that can be changed through natural means; true societal transformation is not a product of human effort alone. In a world increasingly obsessed with self-image and self-gratification, it is essential to recognize the limitations of human-centered approaches to societal change. Like Narcissus, who was consumed by his own reflection, societies often become ensnared in their own self-interests, a byproduct of our fallen nature. True transformation requires a shift in focus from humanity's flawed and self-serving nature to a recognition of and surrender to the Lord.

Compassion and forgiveness are two of the fruits of the Spirit. Compassion is defined as a deep awareness of the suffering of another and a desire to alleviate that suffering. To be compassionate is to be sympathetic and kind. Forgiveness is the act of pardoning an offense and releasing the offender from the obligation of making amends. It is the act of letting go and letting God. The Spirit-filled life is characterized by both compassion and forgiveness. Compassion and forgiveness are natural byproducts of a life in the Spirit.

The absence of natural affection, i.e., compassion, forgiveness, and kindness, are manifestations of life lived in the flesh. Yet even in some churches, these attributes are absent, and before society can experience this transformation, it must begin in the family of God.

Proverbs 3:5-6 (NIV): "Trust in the Lord with all your heart and lean not on your own understanding; in all your ways submit to him, and he will make your paths straight."

For this change to take place in the church and society, repentance and humility before God are indispensable. This requires individuals to acknowledge their shortcomings and wrongdoings, seeking forgiveness and reconciliation. Society as a whole must acknowledge its collective failures and sins, and be willing to turn away from them. Genuine transformation necessitates a willingness to let go of arrogance and embrace humility, recognizing that we are all flawed and in need of the Holy Spirit's guidance.

2 Chronicles 7:14 (NIV): "If my people, who are called by my name, will humble themselves and pray and seek my face and turn from their wicked ways, then I will hear from heaven, and I will forgive their sin and will heal their land."

We open the doors to God's transformative power through repentance and humbling ourselves. Recognizing our limitations and surrendering our will to the Lord's authority provides the foundation for lasting change. God's wisdom and guidance surpass human understanding, offering solutions to societal problems that are beyond our natural capabilities. When society aligns itself with God's principles and seeks His guidance, profound transformation becomes possible.

Isaiah 40:31 (NIV): "But those who hope in the Lord will renew their strength. They will soar on wings like eagles; they will run and not grow weary; they will walk and not faint."

True societal transformation through repentance and humbling ourselves to God also requires deepening our relationship with Him. This entails seeking His presence through prayer, studying His word, and embracing His teachings. By nurturing a connection with God, we as individuals can be inspired, and hopefully, we can inspire others to pursue God, compassion, and express love for one another. This transformation starts within individuals, spreading like ripples in a pond, ultimately leading to a collective change that touches every aspect of society. My hope is that this book will serve as a rock thrown into the pond to start that ripple.

Matthew 22:37-39 (NIV): "Jesus replied: 'Love the Lord your God with all your heart and with all your soul and with all your mind.' This is the first and greatest commandment. And the second is like it: 'Love your neighbor as yourself.'"

True societal transformation is not an outcome of natural means alone. It requires a shift away from self-centeredness and towards repentance and humility before God. As societies increasingly resemble Narcissus, society must recognize its flaws and seek forgiveness through a genuine acknowledgment of its sins. Embracing God's transformative power through deepening our relationship with Him paves the way for lasting change. Only through humility, repentance, and dependence on The Holy Spirit's guidance can society experience the profound transformation it desperately needs. James 4:10 (NIV) says, "Humble yourselves before the Lord, and he will lift you up."

Vulnerability

Intimacy requires humility; deep Intimacy occurs when we surrender to the word, die to self, and serve. Our relationships are shallow because we neither serve nor humble ourselves to be served. Jesus went to wash Peter's feet, and Peter, in pride, said no Lord. What was Peter afraid of? He feared vulnerability; it takes humility to serve and be served, to share your heart and allow someone else to share their heart. Jesus told Peter if you don't allow this act of service, you have no part with me. Deep Intimacy requires the humility of vulnerability. Peter realized immediately he needed to humble himself and receive. Let's read that story: In John 13 No," said Peter, "you shall never wash my feet." Jesus answered, "Unless I wash you, you have no part with me." "Then, Lord," Simon Peter replied, "not just my feet but my hands and my head as well!" Jesus answered, "A person who has had a bath needs only to wash his feet; his whole body is clean. There are no shortcuts to Intimacy with God or the people we are in a relationship with; humility, sacrifice, and vulnerability are necessary. If you have ever had your feet washed by another, it makes you feel exposed, vulnerable, and at the same time close.

We must be willing to humble ourselves and be vulnerable to experience deep Intimacy with our creator and the people we are in relationships with. Peter was afraid of being vulnerable and exposed, but by letting Jesus wash his feet, he experienced deep Intimacy. In the same way, if we are willing to humble ourselves, die to self, and be vulnerable, we will experience Deep Intimacy with our Lord and those we are in relationship with. Intimacy requires humility; it takes courage to expose our hearts and be vulnerable, but when we surrender to the word, die to self, and serve, the rewards are great. We experience Deep Intimacy with our Lord and the people we are in a relationship with. By humbling ourselves and allowing ourselves to be vulnerable, we build trust, strengthen our relationships, and receive God's grace.

Is the idea of being vulnerable something that scares you? It scares many people because with vulnerability there is always the risk of being taken advantage of and hurt. But without that possibility, there is no love, as love requires sacrifice, and sacrifice is often painful. Jesus paved the way when he sacrificed everything for us. We caused him great pain, but the fruit of his sacrifice is eternal; we must willingly serve others and allow ourselves to be served. Embrace vulnerability. It can be frightening to reveal your true self to someone, particularly if you have been concealing it for a long time. Narcissistic individuals aim to manipulate their environment to avoid exposure and vulnerability. They live in constant fear and respond aggressively toward anyone threatening their feelings of security, and to the narcissist, intimacy is a threat. The individuals affected by them, who are in a relationship with a narcissist, constantly question why their loved ones choose not to reciprocate their love. In this book, I extensively explore the complex nature of narcissistic abuse, delving into its multiple dimensions and offering a way toward liberation for both the victim and the narcissist.

CHAPTER ONE

UNDERSTANDING NARCISSISM

Narcissism, a term frequently used in psychology and often depicted negatively in popular culture, represents a character trait characterized by an excessive focus on oneself, an insatiable need for admiration, and a lack of empathy for others. To overcome narcissism, it is essential first to comprehend its roots and manifestations.

The Seeds of Narcissism

Narcissism can trace its origins to a variety of factors, including early childhood experiences, upbringing, and societal influences. Some individuals may develop narcissistic tendencies as a defense mechanism, shielding themselves from emotional pain or insecurity. A dysfunctional, abusive, or alcoholic family upbringing can lead to a fear of vulnerability and other traits associated with narcissism. Narcissistic traits often develop as a result of childhood trauma or neglect, as well as a lack of secure attachment in childhood or early adulthood. In such families, a child may have difficulty developing a sense of self-worth or self-esteem and may become overly self-centered or defensive to protect themselves from further hurt or rejection. As a result, these individuals may develop a fear of vulnerability, leading to the narcissistic traits seen in adulthood.

The False Self

One of the core elements of narcissism is the cultivation of a false self, a carefully constructed facade designed to project an image of superiority and invincibility. This false self often masks underlying feelings of vulnerability and inadequacy.

The Narcissistic Spectrum

Loving ourselves exists on a spectrum, ranging from healthy self-esteem to pathological narcissism. It is crucial to differentiate between healthy self-confidence and the destructive patterns of narcissism when assessing ourselves or others. Loving ourselves means accepting ourselves for who we are, flaws and all. It means taking responsibility for one's own actions and being kind to oneself. This type of self-love is healthy and can actually help us to be more loving to others. When we love ourselves, we can better recognize our own needs and be more attentive to the needs of others. It also helps us to be more compassionate and understanding of those around us. Loving oneself can also help us build strong relationships with those around us, as we can better connect with others when we are at peace with ourselves.

The Spiritual Implications

From a spiritual perspective, narcissism represents a deviation from the path of humility, selflessness, and genuine love advocated by the Word of God. It can hinder our ability to experience God's grace and cultivate meaningful relationships with others. It is a byproduct of the fallen nature.

Breaking Free from Narcissism

Overcoming narcissism is a challenging but transformative journey. It requires honest self-reflection, acknowledging our tendencies, and a willingness to seek healing and transformation. Embracing vulnerability becomes a pivotal step on this path.

Aligning with Christ's Example

"Let each of you look not only to his own interests but also to the interests of others." (Philippians 2:4, ESV) In Philippians 2:4 also, we find guidance on how to combat narcissism, a call to shift our focus from self-centeredness to concern for the well-being of others. Christ's example of humility and selflessness is the ultimate model for breaking free from narcissistic tendencies. God the Son became a servant; think about the humility it takes to do something like that, the creator of the universe serving his creation because he loves them.

Understanding narcissism is the first step toward healing and transformation. It involves recognizing the roots and manifestations of narcissistic tendencies in ourselves or others. By aligning with Christ's teachings on humility and selflessness, we embark on a journey that leads to a life marked by authenticity, compassion, and a deeper connection with God and those around us.

1.1 Biblical reference to narcissistic behavior.

In 2 Timothy 3:2, it is foretold that in the last days, perilous times shall come. One aspect of these perilous times is emphasized in the biblical reference to narcissistic behavior. The verse states, "For men shall be lovers of their own selves." It's interesting how the

Bible often has timeless wisdom that can be applied to our lives today. This behavior sounds pretty familiar. We see it all around us: the growing trend of self-centeredness and narcissism. Men becoming lovers of their own selves!

2 Timothy 3:2 (NIV): "People will be lovers of themselves, lovers of money, boastful, proud, abusive, disobedient to their parents, ungrateful, unholy."

Narcissistic behavior is all about excessive self-love and an obsession with one's own needs, wants, and desires. It's like being trapped in a little bubble where the only thing that matters is you. And let's be honest, we've probably all encountered someone like that at some point in our lives.

In today's world of social media and constant self-promotion, it's no wonder that narcissism seems to be on the rise. People are more focused on crafting the perfect image of themselves online, seeking validation through likes and followers. It's a never-ending pursuit of self-worth through external validation.

Proverbs 16:18 (NIV): "Pride goes before destruction, a haughty spirit before a fall."

But here's the thing - being self-centered isn't a healthy or fulfilling way to live. True happiness and fulfillment come from connecting with others, showing empathy, and being part of something bigger than ourselves. It's about finding meaning beyond just our own needs and desires. True fulfillment is a byproduct of being heavenly-minded, of having an eternal perspective and purpose.

1 Timothy 6:6-11(NIV) But godliness with contentment is great gain. For we brought nothing into the world, and we can take

nothing out of it. But if we have food and clothing, we will be content with that.

So, while the rise of narcissism may be one aspect of the perilous or difficult times foretold in the Bible, it's also a reminder for us to reflect on our own behavior. Maybe it's time to step back from self-centeredness and focus on building genuine connections with others and with the Lord because, in the end, that's what truly matters.

Matthew 16:26 (NIV): "What good will it be for someone to gain the whole world, yet forfeit their soul? Or what can anyone give in exchange for their soul?"

Throughout the Bible, there are several examples and stories that illustrate the detrimental effects of narcissistic behavior. One such example is the story of King Saul in the Old Testament. God anointed Saul to be King, and Saul had the potential to do great things and bring lasting change to the nation of Israel, but because of his narcissistic tendencies, he refused to submit to God. God sent Samuel to rebuke him, and instead of repenting, he lied and said I did obey; he had not; he had only partly obeyed, which is not obedience. Then he said, I have sinned: yet honor me now, I pray thee, before the elders of my people, and before Israel, and turn again with me, that I may worship the LORD thy God. 1 Samuel 15:30. Instead of grieving over his sin and being concerned about getting right with God, Saul was worried about how he looked in front of the people, outward appearances, keeping up the facade, he said," honor me in front of the people. "

1 Samuel 15:27 (NIV): "As Samuel turned to leave, Saul caught hold of the hem of his robe, and it tore."

He grabbed the robe of the prophet and tried to manipulate him. He wanted the prophet to perpetrate a pretense. Saul started his reign with humility, but as his power grew, so did his narcissism. He became consumed with jealousy and pride, leading him to disregard God's instructions and ultimately lose his kingship.

1 Samuel 15:23 (NIV): "For rebellion is like the sin of divination, and arrogance like the evil of idolatry."

Why does the bible call rebellion, divination, and idolatry? Divination is a type of witchcraft; in ancient times, divination was used to control people. When we try to control or manipulate God or the people whom God has placed in authority over us, we assume his position, making ourselves out to be God, which is the idolatry of self-worship. Saul's rebellion was a byproduct of his narcissistic mindset; instead of obeying God, he was trying to manipulate God. Satan was cast out of heaven for trying to do the same thing; instead of obeying God, he wanted to rule over him. Christians do the same thing when trying to manipulate the word of God instead of observing it. The story of Saul highlights the significance of self-awareness and the dangers of narcissism. It reminds us that our relationship with God is not transactional, based on appearances, performance, and manipulation, but based on love. We don't obey God to earn his love; he loved us when we were sinners and proved it by dying for us. We obey God because we love him; he said," If you love me, you will keep my commandments. Love is a deeply personal and transformative journey where we give ourselves freely and openly unconditionally. When we decide to obey God only if he does what we want, we behave narcissisticly toward him. We can cultivate a healthy and fulfilling relationship with God through genuine repentance (being honest about our sins and shortcomings and a willingness to change), humility, and a sincere desire to seek God's will. This same principle applies in our human relationships: honesty, vulnerability, and willingness to change, and we sincerely seek to serve and love, which will create some powerful relational bonds.

Psalm 51:17 (NIV): "My sacrifice, O God, is a broken spirit; a broken and contrite heart you, God, will not despise."

Saul's request for Samuel to walk with him before the people reveals his inclination toward image management rather than inner transformation. His primary concern seemed to be preserving his position and the respect of his subjects rather than genuinely seeking guidance or embracing a humble attitude before God.

Proverbs 3:5-6 (NIV): "Trust in the Lord with all your heart and lean not on your own understanding; in all your ways submit to him, and he will make your paths straight."

The story of Saul serves as a reminder that true fulfillment and success can only be found when we align ourselves with God's calling and prioritize our relationship with Him above all else.

Micah 6:8 (NIV): "He has shown you, O mortal, what is good. And what does the Lord require of you? To act justly and to love mercy and to walk humbly with your God."

In 2 Samuel 1:17-27 and 1 Samuel 15:27, the tragic downfall of Saul is depicted, as he lost all connection to his calling and relationship with God. Saul was anointed as the first king of Israel, chosen by God to lead His people with wisdom and righteousness. However, Saul's relationship with God deteriorated over time due to disobedience and self-centeredness. He became more concerned with his desires and personal agenda than following God's instructions. As a result, Saul lost touch with his divine calling, and his connection with God was stripped away. His narcissism drove his actions, often leading to a life filled with broken relationships with God and those around him. Despite God's rejection, Saul clung to the throne and did not give it up. He became increasingly paranoid, and his actions showed a lack of faith in God. He sought out a witch to get a prophecy, which was an act of rebellion against God. He commanded his people to kill innocent people in his pursuit of David and had Jonathan, his own son, arrested for treason. Saul's refusal to seek God and obey His commands led to his downfall, and in the end, he died by his own sword. King Saul is a reminder of the consequences of disobeying God's commands and the importance of having faith and trust in God's will. God does not reject us when we fail, but He does expect us to repent and seek His forgiveness, something Saul refused to do. Saul's story is a lesson for us to learn from and to remember that God's mercy is always available and that we must rely on Him in all things.

Psalm 51:10 (NIV): "Create in me a pure heart, O God, and renew a steadfast spirit within me."

Saul's tragic downfall serves as a cautionary tale about the consequences of self-centeredness and ignoring God's will. His pursuit of power and personal satisfaction blinded him to the importance of obeying God's commands. Saul lost God's favor and guidance in his disobedience, leading to his ultimate demise. His life became a series of broken relationships as he failed to nurture and value the people God had placed in his life. The story of Saul serves as a reminder that true fulfillment and success can only be found when we align ourselves with God's calling and prioritize our relationship with Him above all else. David's cry was, Lord, create in me a clean heart, a right heart, a steadfast heart; he had failures also, but his hearts desire was to get right with God, intimacy with the Lord and others.

Isaiah 2:22 (NIV): "Stop trusting in mere humans, who have but a breath in their nostrils. Why hold them in esteem?"

Another biblical character who displayed narcissistic tendencies was King Nebuchadnezzar in the Book of Daniel. Nebuchadnezzar was a powerful ruler, but his arrogance and self-adulation caused him to ignore the warnings of the prophet Daniel. He built statues of himself and instructed the populace to bow down and worship them, and if they refused, they would be put to death. He even started to take credit for what the Lord had accomplished. This behavior angered the Lord, and As a consequence, he was stripped of his sanity and forced to live like a wild animal until he humbled himself before God.

Daniel 4:31-33 The same hour was the thing fulfilled upon Nebuchadnezzar: and he was driven from men, and did eat grass as oxen, and his body was wet with the dew of heaven, till his hairs were grown like eagles' feathers, and his nails like birds' claws."

Nebuchadnezzar was so prideful that he thought all creation should bow down to him; this led him to a pride-induced delusional decision to construct statues, demonstrating his overwhelming need for validation and adoration. His obsession with his own glory closed his eyes to the consequences of his actions and the suffering he caused his subjects. What disturbs me is that he was not even bothered by the loss of life and disrespecting the Lord. When there is an accumulation of wealth, position, and status, narcissists believe others are beneath them and that they have the right to treat them as they would like. The only thing that made him repent and acknowledge the Lord was his loss of sanity.

Daniel 4:37 (NIV): "Now I, Nebuchadnezzar, praise and exalt and glorify the King of heaven, because everything he does is right and all his ways are just. And those who walk in pride he is able to be humble."

When narcissists are confronted with their behavior, if they repent, you will see a dramatic transformation; if they don't repent, they will usually get worse and worse—a type of insanity. If you are going to confront a violent narcissist, it is a good idea to have someone with you.

Proverbs 11:2 (NIV): "When pride comes, then comes disgrace, but with humility comes wisdom."

It was through this humbling experience that Nebuchadnezzar learned a valuable lesson. When his sanity was restored, he acknowledged the sovereignty of God and humbled himself, recognizing that it is God who holds ultimate power and authority.

1 Peter 5:6 (NIV): "Humble yourselves, therefore, under God's mighty hand, that he may lift you up in due time."

In the New Testament, the parable of the prodigal son can also be seen as an illustration of narcissistic behavior. The prodigal son demanded his share of the inheritance and left his family, squandering his wealth on selfish desires. Only after hitting rock bottom did he realize the error of his ways and return humbly to his father. His father eventually blessed and forgave him; humility and recognizing his failure was the path to that blessed redemption.

Luke 15:17-18 (NIV): "When he came to his senses, he said, 'How many of my father's hired servants have food to spare, and here I am starving to death! I will set out and go back to my father and say to him: Father, I have sinned against heaven and against you.'"

These biblical examples and stories warn against the dangers of narcissistic behavior. They demonstrate how self-centeredness and pride can lead to destruction and separation from God. As believers, we must be aware of these traits and strive to cultivate humility and genuine love for others, especially in these difficult times.

Philippians 2:3-4 (NIV): "Do nothing out of selfish ambition or vain conceit. Rather, in humility, value others above yourselves, not looking to your own interests but each of you to the interests of the others."

The story of Absalom, the son of King David, is yet another example of narcissism in the Bible. Absalom's sense of entitlement and self-importance originated from his being considered exceptionally beautiful. The verse from 2 Samuel 14:25 highlights that people constantly praised Absalom for his remarkable appearance, to the point that he started to believe his own press. When I was growing up, we used to call that the big head, a swollen sense of self-importance. This constant affirmation created a strong delusion in Absalom's mind, convincing him that his beauty made him superior to others. It fueled his entitlement and planted the seeds of an inflated ego within him.

2 Samuel 14:25 (NIV): "In all Israel, there was not a man so highly praised for his handsome appearance as Absalom. From the top of his head to the sole of his foot, there was no blemish in him."

As time went on, Absalom's sense of entitlement grew even stronger. He began to believe that his beauty entitled him not only to the admiration of others but also to positions of power and authority. This inflated perception of self-importance led him to rebel against his father, King David, attempting to seize the kingdom for himself. Absalom's strong delusion of entitlement distorted his understanding of reality, causing him to believe that he was the rightful heir to the throne, even though this was not the case. His self-importance blinded him to the consequences of his actions, ultimately leading to his downfall. His narcissistic behavior ultimately led to his demise, and he was killed in battle.

Proverbs 16:18 (NIV): "Pride goes before destruction, a haughty spirit before a fall."

Not only did Absalom's narcissism stem from his perceived physical superiority, but it also grew through his father's indulgence and lack of consequences for his actions. Absalom realized that he could manipulate situations and exploit his position as the favored son, using his looks and charm to gain favor and influence, and this led him to make decisions based solely on his desires, disregarding the welfare of others and the consequences that his actions might have.

As the story unfolds, we see Absalom's narcissism and self-centeredness lead to a deepening sense of entitlement. He covered his father's throne and was willing to do whatever it took to seize power for himself, including manipulating the people's hearts, undermining David's authority, and ultimately staging a rebellion against his father.

Proverbs 29:23 (NIV): "Pride brings a person low, but the lowly in spirit gain honor."

Absalom's narcissistic tendencies blinded him to the consequences of his actions. He failed to consider the destruction he was causing to his family and the more expansive kingdom. His self-absorption prevented him from truly understanding his choices' impact on others' lives. Pursuing power and validation consumed him to the point of losing all sense of empathy and compassion.

Proverbs 21:4 (NIV): "Haughty eyes and a proud heart—the unplowed field of the wicked, produce sin."

The tragic downfall of Absalom serves as a cautionary tale, reminding us of the destructive power of narcissism. It serves as a reminder to be aware of the dangers of excessive self-focus, as it can blind us to reality.

1 Peter 5:5 (NIV): "All of you, clothe yourselves with humility toward one another, because, 'God opposes the proud but shows favor to the humble.'"

1.2 Defining Narcissism and Its Characteristics

From a psychological perspective and character analysis, narcissism is a personality trait characterized by an inflated sense of self-importance, an excessive need for attention and admiration, and a lack of empathy for others; from a biblically, it is the fruit of living in the flesh or a fleshly mentality. People who exhibit narcissistic tendencies often have an exaggerated view of their abilities and achievements and believe they are entitled to special treatment and privileges. The term "narcissism" originates from Greek mythology, where Narcissus, a young hunter known for his exceptional beauty, became so infatuated with his own reflection in a pool of water that he eventually died by drowning while trying to embrace his own image.

One of the key characteristics of narcissism is an excessive need for admiration and attention. Individuals with narcissistic tendencies crave constant praise and validation from others, and they often go to great lengths to seek out admiration and recognition. They may engage in grandiose behaviors or boast about their accomplishments, seeking to be the center of attention in social settings.

This characteristic can be linked to biblical principles. For instance, Proverbs 27:2 (NIV) warns against self-praise and the pursuit of attention: "Let someone else praise you, and not your own mouth; an outsider, and not your own lips."

Another prominent characteristic of narcissism is a lack of empathy. Individuals with narcissistic personality traits have difficulty understanding and relating to the emotions and experiences of others. They may appear cold and indifferent to the struggles of those around them, as they are primarily focused on their own needs and desires.

This lack of empathy is reminiscent of passages such as Philippians 2:3-4 (NIV): "Do nothing out of selfish ambition or vain conceit. Rather, in humility, value others above yourselves, not looking to your own interests but each of you to the interests of the others."

Narcissistic individuals typically have an exaggerated sense of self-importance. They believe that they are superior to others and deserve special treatment; this can lead to a sense of entitlement and a disregard for the rights and feelings of others. They may approach relationships with a transactional mindset, viewing others as objects to serve their needs.

This behavior contradicts biblical teachings, such as Galatians 5:13 (NIV): "You, my brothers and sisters, were called to be free. But do not use your freedom to indulge the flesh; rather, serve one another humbly in love."

Furthermore, individuals with narcissistic tendencies often have fragile self-esteem that is easily threatened. Despite projecting an image of confidence and superiority, they are hypersensitive to criticism or rejection. Any perceived slight or challenge to their self-image can result in aggressive or defensive reactions as they struggle to maintain their idealized self-image. This sensitivity to criticism is reminiscent of the wisdom in Proverbs 15:1 (NIV): "A gentle answer turns away wrath, but a harsh word stirs up anger." With the narcissist, any rebuke, even gentle rebuke, is heard as harsh

Recognizing these characteristics and their biblical contrasts can help in understanding and navigating relationships with individuals who display narcissistic traits.

Exploring the Traits and Behaviors Exhibited by Narcissists

One crucial aspect to consider when examining the traits and behaviors exhibited by narcissists is how they treat people. Narcissists tend to prioritize themselves above all else, often demonstrating a lack of empathy and exploiting others for personal gain. They view interpersonal relationships as opportunities to assert their superiority and control, frequently engaging in manipulative tactics to achieve their desired outcomes.

Narcissists often treat people as mere tools or pawns in their game of self-gratification. Initially, they may be charming and charismatic, but their interactions are often superficial and insincere. They exhibit a pattern of using others to boost their ego and inflate their own self-importance, disregarding the needs and feelings of those around them. Their actions are driven by a constant desire for attention and admiration, which is a defining characteristic of narcissistic behavior.

Narcissists have a tendency to display an extreme sense of entitlement. They expect others to cater to their needs and desires without question or hesitation. They believe they deserve special treatment simply by virtue of their perceived superiority. This sense of entitlement often leads to a disregard for boundaries and an expectation of constant validation and attention, which can be emotionally draining and exhausting for those who interact with them.

This attitude contradicts biblical principles, as 1 Corinthians 10:24 (NIV) advises: "No one should seek their own good, but the good of others."

Another key behavior exhibited by narcissists is their tendency to manipulate and exploit others. They are skilled at manipulating people's emotions and opinions to further their agenda; this may involve gaslighting. Gaslighting is twisting reality to make others doubt their own perceptions or experiences. Additionally, they may engage in manipulation tactics such as guilt-tripping, playing the victim, or employing charm and flattery to win people over.

This behavior starkly contrasts the biblical call for honesty and integrity, as Ephesians 4:25 (NIV) states: "Therefore each of you must put off falsehood and speak truthfully to your neighbor, for we are all members of one body."

They often struggle with displaying genuine empathy towards others. While they may possess an intellectual understanding of emotions, they are typically incapable of experiencing real empathy. They may mimic empathetic behaviors to manipulate others or gain their trust, but their lack of genuine concern for others is evident. This inability to empathize can cause immense harm to those who have relationships with narcissists, as their emotional needs are often neglected or dismissed.

Narcissists' behavior towards others is characterized by self-centeredness that permeates their interactions. They exploit, manipulate, and disregard the needs and boundaries of others while prioritizing their desires and wants. Recognizing these traits and behaviors can be crucial in protecting oneself from the potential harm that can be caused by interacting with a narcissist.

Discussing the Lack of Natural Affection and Emotional Reciprocity in Their Relationships

When it comes to relationships, such as those with a spouse, children, friends, or coworkers, a lack of natural affection and emotional reciprocity can be evident in the behaviors and expectations of narcissists. Narcissists are individuals who have an excessive sense of self-importance and a deep need for admiration and attention. This self-centeredness often leads to a neglect of others' emotional needs and an inability to form deep and meaningful connections.

A narcissist may lack the ability to truly love their partner. Their focus tends to be on their own needs and desires, and they often expect their partner to cater to their every whim. This lack of emotional reciprocity can lead to a one-sided and unfulfilling relationship, as the narcissist cannot provide the emotional support and understanding crucial for intimacy.

Similarly, with children, a narcissistic parent may struggle to show genuine love and affection towards their offspring. Their focus may often be on how their children reflect their image and accomplishments rather than on the child's individuality and emotional needs. This lack of natural affection can significantly impact a child's development and result in feelings of neglect and emotional instability.

In friendships, narcissists may struggle to form deep and meaningful connections. They may use their friends for personal gain or seek constant validation and attention while rarely reciprocating these emotions. This one-sided dynamic can lead to a sense of emptiness and dissatisfaction for both parties involved, as genuine connection requires mutual care and consideration.

Even within a professional setting, narcissists can exhibit a lack of natural affection and emotional reciprocity towards their coworkers. They may view their colleagues as competition or as tools to enhance their own status and success. This self-centered approach can create a toxic work environment where cooperation and collaboration are undermined, and the emotional well-being of those involved is compromised.

Cultivating emotional connections requires understanding shared vulnerability, empathy, and genuine care; qualities narcissists typically do not possess. However, these attributes can be cultivated by walking in the Spirit, as they are the fruit of the Spirit. Narcissists can sometimes make excellent employees as they can be hard workers and sacrifice to be seen, and many jobs do not require intimacy or close interaction. However, the more successful, the harder it is to breach the wall they have constructed around themselves.

Relevant Bible Verses:

- **Proverbs 27:2 (NIV):** "Let someone else praise you, and not your own mouth; an outsider, and not your own lips."

- **Philippians 2:3-4 (NIV):** "Do nothing out of selfish ambition or vain conceit. Rather, in humility, value others above yourselves, not looking to your own interests but each of you to the interests of the others."

- **Galatians 5:13 (NIV):** "You, my brothers and sisters, were called to be free. But do not use your freedom to indulge the flesh; rather, serve one another humbly in love."

- **Proverbs 15:1 (NIV):** "A gentle answer turns away wrath, but a harsh word stirs up anger."

- **1 Corinthians 10:24 (NIV):** "No one should seek their own good, but the good of others."

- **Ephesians 4:25 (NIV):** "Therefore each of you must put off falsehood and speak truthfully to your neighbor, for we are all members of one body."

1.3 Highlight the impact of being in a relationship with a narcissist.

One of the most significant aspects of such a relationship is the absence of reciprocity and intimacy. Narcissists are so focused on themselves and their own needs that they often disregard the feelings and desires of their partner. This lack of emotional connection can leave the other person feeling unheard, unimportant, and unloved. A relationship with a narcissist can often feel like unrequited love.

During the 80's, there was a phrase, "Romancing the Stone. "The term 'romancing the stone' has come to refer to any situation in which one attempts to win something of great value, usually through charm and wit, yet it remains unattainable. A relationship with a narcissist has been compared to romancing a stone. Intimacy may seem like it is within reach, and at the same time, it seems as though it is unattainable, and even if you get the stone, it is devoid of reciprocity, intimacy, and genuine love. The frustration of constantly giving without receiving in return can take a toll on one's emotional well-being. It is crucial for individuals in such relationships to recognize the signs of narcissism and seek support to break free from this cycle of unrequited love. The frustration of it all stems from the constant imbalance in the relationship. While one partner may give their all, the narcissist remains self-absorbed, rarely showing genuine care or concern. They may appear charming initially, but their selfish nature becomes apparent as the relationship progresses. The non-narcissistic partner may find themselves constantly trying to please and fulfill the needs of the narcissist, only to be met with indifference or even manipulation.

Emotional and physical intimacy is essential for a healthy and fulfilling relationship. However, in a relationship with a narcissist, true intimacy is rarely experienced. Narcissists struggle to empathize with others and often lack the emotional depth necessary for a meaningful connection; this leaves their partner feeling emotionally deprived and alone, as if they are constantly trying to reach an unattainable goal.

The lack of reciprocity and intimacy in a relationship with a narcissist can lead to feelings of unrequited love. The non-narcissistic partner may pour their heart and soul into the relationship, hoping that their efforts will be reciprocated. However, the narcissist's focus on themselves prevents them from truly loving their partner in the way they deserve. This imbalance can result in a profound sense of disappointment and longing for a love that may never be fully realized; this is especially difficult for married people. An unmarried person can move on. That's why God commands married believers to meet their mate's emotional and physical needs. It is sexual and emotional sin not to reciprocate in a marriage, to reap and not sow. Reaping and sowing are what farmers do every day; they plant seed, and when it grows, they get to eat the fruit of their labor and hard work. If a thief comes into the field and steals the fruit, he has reaped but has not sowed or planted anything, making him a thief. That principle applies in relationships. You are in sin if you are not sowing love, physical and emotional affection, and kindness into your mate.

1 Corinthians 7:5 Do not deprive each other of sexual relations unless you both agree to refrain from sexual intimacy for a limited time so you can give yourselves more completely to prayer. Afterward, you should come together again so Satan won't be able to tempt you because of your lack of self-control.

Depriving your mate during marriage is a horrible thing to do. The Puritans considered you not to be saved if you frequently denied your mate emotional or physical affection. Most people would say why? It doesn't seem like a big deal, but it is a big deal. The Lord says in the word that when we deny our mates, we give place to the devil. The word place means home or a doorway; when you deprive your mate, it's like you opened the door and invited the devil into your and your mate's hearts; you have put a target on their back. The scripture says, do not deprive them so you or your mate won't be tempted to go outside the marriage to meet the need. I heard a woman who did not want to show her husband physical or emotional affection talking about her husband; she said," he was a Christian for years before we got married, and if he didn't sleep around when he was a single Christian he would be fine, he just needs self-control. Her husband was strong in the Lord in every other area but struggled with lust, something he did not struggle with before marriage. It's easier to be a single Christian living for the Lord and stay pure than to be married to someone who denies you physical and emotional affection and remains pure. If you are a single Christian male or female, you do not expect marital, physical, or emotional intimacy, so you keep your heart on the things of the Lord. You don't go there in your heart. If you're married, you might spend part of your day thinking about your wife or husband, excited about coming home and spending your night in physical and emotional intimacy. If you are married to a narcissist, you can go home, and your mate frequently tells you no to both. The problem is that the need doesn't go away just because your mate said no; it intensifies. Why do you think so many married people are falling into sin? We have given the enemy access. That person is in danger, so God warned the believer not to do it. If you're in that situation, God can provide you with grace, but it will be a ferocious battle. Sex and emotional intimacy were both given by God to bind us together. During sex, touch, and emotional interactions with your mate, Oxytocin is released; It is frequently referred to as the "love hormone." It binds us together so that we long for each other's touch.

Passive Response

A great example of what it's like to be in a narcissistic relationship in the Bible is the story of Ahab and Jezebel; it gives us insight into the long-term effects of being in these relationships. Let's preface this story by saying that Jezebel is the extreme case, not the norm.

Jezebel was a well-known biblical character with qualities that epitomized the narcissistic personality. Jezebel was the wife of King Ahab and hailed from a pagan background, where she worshiped false idols. Her influence over Ahab was palpable, exploiting his weakness and manipulating him to fulfill her desires. This power dynamic mirrored the traits commonly associated with narcissistic individuals.

In a relationship with a narcissist like Jezebel, one can expect a constant need for attention and admiration. Jezebel's voracious appetite for adulation or admiration was evident in her actions, as she repeatedly sought grandiose displays of power and control. This insatiable thirst for recognition often led to acts of manipulation, deceit, and even violence. Her life's mission was to stop Israel from worshiping God. She threatened and killed the prophets. Narcissists don't care about God's will; they want what they want. In fact, they openly oppose God's purposes because to obey God, they have to relinquish control. You can give them scripture all day long in context, and they will say, my bible says something different, or I don't believe that. Even if you tell the narcissist, look according to the rules of grammar, your bible does say what my bible says, they will reject what you're saying. The laws of grammar don't matter to a narcissist. I remember many years ago, I was on deployment in the desert with my unit, and I noticed a guy reading a Playboy magazine in the front seat of the cargo truck, so I decided to witness him; he told me I am born again and serving God, I told him, you're not in the front seat of this truck, or something along those lines, and shared with him all the scriptures dealing with lust. No matter how many scriptures I shared, he did not hear them, and he went right back to reading those magazines. It wasn't information he lacked; he lacked the will to change. I could have read the whole bible to him. Jezebel had the same problem; she knew the truth; the prophets spoke the word plainly, and she had them slaughtered. When you want to do wrong, you don't want to hear the truth; it bothers your conscience. Narcissists reject the truth; if you tell anyone what they are doing or try to get help, they will often try to discredit or lie about you. I knew one young woman in a relationship with a narcissist; she told me he turned her whole family against her, not his family, but hers. They are skillful manipulators; you have got to be skilled to turn someone's family against them. If the person is a violent narcissist, they may try to hurt you; if you need to confront them, do it over the phone, and if you feel unsafe or in danger of physical harm, leave; the Lord does not want you in that type of situation.

The same is true if they are trying to goad you into behaving inappropriately; some narcissists will physically or emotionally abuse you until they entice you into inappropriate behavior, even sin. They want you to strike back or act out. They believe by doing so, they now have a justification for their emotional detachment and other behaviors. That's what happened to Ahab. The Bible says Jezebel stirred him up, which means she vexed and wore him down until she got her way.

1 Kings 21:25 KJV: "But there was none like unto Ahab, who did sell himself to work wickedness in the sight of the LORD, whom Jezebel his wife stirred up."

Being involved with a narcissist like Jezebel can be emotionally draining and psychologically damaging. Their need for superiority and dominance often results in the devaluation of those around them. They take advantage of others' vulnerability to further their agenda without regard for the consequences or the well-being of their victims.

Jezebel's story is a stark reminder of narcissistic individuals' devastating effects on our lives. Her narcissism was so severe that she killed people to get her way and to feed her lust for power. Ahab, her husband, became increasingly passive and powerless in their relationship. Over time, Jezebel's manipulative and domineering nature consistently vexed Ahab and the entire nation under their rule. Think about this for a minute; he is the King, allowing her to kill God's people. And that's why Ahab was eventually dealt with as well. God judged them both. Don't let the narcissist goad you into sin; fight for your relationship and stay strong in the Lord, pray in the Spirit, ask for the Lord to heal them of spiritual blindness, read the word, and ask for help. God has to open their eyes.

David's Dilemma: David was not married to a narcissist; he was employed by one. In the Bible, in 1 Samuel 19, we learn about the relationship between David and Saul. David had served Saul faithfully, winning numerous victories on his behalf and becoming a trusted and beloved figure in the kingdom. However, as David started to achieve success, Saul's narcissistic tendencies became evident through his jealousy, manipulation, and obsession with maintaining his power and control. Despite David's loyalty and dedication, Saul's insecurities led him to plot against David's life.

In 1 Samuel 19, we see Saul's attempts to kill David. He first throws a spear at him while David plays the harp for him, trying to calm his troubled spirit. David manages to escape, and Saul repeatedly sends messengers and even his son, Jonathan, to try and take David's life.

Throughout this ordeal, David consistently shows respect and honor towards Saul, refusing to retaliate or harm the king he once served with great devotion. Instead, David seeks refuge with Jonathan, who becomes a loyal friend and ally.

David's experiences with Saul highlight the destructive nature of a narcissistic employer. He faces constant threats to his life, loses his position, and must continuously be on guard. However, his response serves as an example of navigating difficult relationships – with humility, integrity, and a reliance on God's guidance.

1 Samuel 19:1-2 NIV: "Saul told his son Jonathan and all the attendants to kill David. But Jonathan had taken a great liking to David and warned him, 'My father Saul is looking for a chance to kill you. Be on your guard tomorrow morning; go into hiding and stay there.'"

The story of David and Saul highlights the idea that those driven by narcissism often struggle to see the potential and success in others. It also demonstrates the importance of remaining true to oneself and pursuing one's dreams despite the resistance met by narcissistic individuals. David's unwavering love and determination to fulfill his destiny serve as a testament to the power of perseverance and the triumph of good over evil. David stayed the course, and the Lord exalted him and made him King, from shepherd to King.

The Narcissist Struggles With These Relational Skills:

The missing kiss: Fear of intimacy and a lack of transparency are common traits observed in narcissists, which often leads them to avoid the act of kissing in their relationships. For narcissists, the concept of intimacy and transparency can trigger deep-seated fears that they are reluctant to confront or reveal to others. Kissing symbolizes a level of vulnerability that narcissists are uncomfortable with, as it demands genuine emotional connection and trust.

This reluctance to engage in kissing can be related to biblical principles. For instance, Ephesians 5:25 (NIV) is written, "Husbands, love your wives, just as Christ loved the church and gave himself up for her." Kissing is often seen as a physical expression of love and intimacy within a marriage. For narcissists who struggle with genuine emotional connection, this act of selfless love and vulnerability can be challenging to embrace.

Often, Narcissists are driven by an intense need for control and maintaining a facade of superiority. With its inherent intimacy, kissing can break down these walls and expose their vulnerabilities. This fear of losing control prevents them from engaging in this act of closeness. By avoiding kissing, narcissists can attempt to preserve their carefully crafted image and avoid any potential exposure of their true selves.

Another reason why narcissists avoid kissing is their fear of becoming dependent on someone else. Intimacy often requires a level of dependency and reliance on another person. Narcissists fear losing their sense of independence and becoming emotionally reliant on their partner. They view dependency as a weakness, so they avoid actions like kissing that could potentially lead to emotional dependence.

Narcissists rarely form genuine emotional connections with others. Their relationships tend to be superficial, centered around their needs and desires. Kissing requires a level of emotional investment and empathy, qualities that narcissists often lack. They prioritize their gratification above all else, making it difficult for them to empathize with their partner's emotions and engage in activities reinforcing emotional connection.

Narcissists also fear the vulnerability that comes with open displays of affection. Expressing love and affection through kissing requires a level of vulnerability that does not align with their desire to maintain a strong, invulnerable persona. By avoiding physical displays of affection like kissing, they can protect themselves from potential hurt or rejection.

They are often more interested in power dynamics than genuine affection. Kissing is an act that allows for mutual vulnerability, equalizing the power dynamic in a relationship. Narcissists thrive on maintaining a power imbalance and avoiding a level playing field. Thus, they withhold physical affection like kissing to maintain control and keep their partner in a subordinate position.

The fear of intimacy and transparency lies at the core of why narcissists often avoid kissing their mates. This fear stems from their need for control, avoidance of dependency, lack of genuine emotional connection, fear of vulnerability, and desire to maintain power dynamics. As a result, narcissists struggle to engage in acts of physical affection that require emotional vulnerability, such as kissing, in their relationships.

CHAPTER TWO
IDENTIFYING THE NARCISSIST

Identifying a narcissist can be a challenging but crucial endeavor, as it allows you to protect yourself and navigate relationships with wisdom and discernment. Narcissists often display a range of distinct characteristics and behaviors that, when recognized, can serve as red flags. Here, we'll delve into how to identify a narcissist and consider relevant Bible verses that offer guidance in this process.

- **Excessive Need for Admiration:** One of the primary traits of a narcissist is an insatiable need for admiration and attention. They often fish for compliments and constantly seek praise from those around them. This behavior can be a manifestation of their deep-seated insecurity and desire to maintain their inflated self-image. Proverbs 27:21 (NIV) warns, "The crucible for silver and the furnace for gold, but people are tested by their praise."

- **Lack of Empathy:** Narcissists frequently struggle with empathy, finding it challenging to understand or care about the emotions of others. They may appear indifferent to the suffering or feelings of those around them, as they are primarily focused on their own needs. Philippians 2:4 (NIV) advises, "Not looking to your own interests but each of you to the interests of the others."

- **Sense of Entitlement:** Narcissists often believe they are entitled to special treatment and privileges. They may disregard the rights and feelings of others and expect constant validation. This sense of entitlement is contrary to the biblical principle of humility. James 4:6 (NIV) says, "But he gives us more grace. That is why Scripture says: 'God opposes the proud but shows favor to the humble.'"

- **Manipulative Behavior:** Narcissists are skilled manipulators who use various tactics to control and exploit others. Their tactics include anything from gaslighting to guilt-tripping to playing the victim. Ephesians 4:25 (NIV) encourages honesty and integrity in our interactions: "Therefore each of you must put off falsehood and speak truthfully to your neighbor."

- **Fragile Self-Esteem:** Despite projecting an image of confidence, narcissists often have fragile self-esteem that is easily wounded. They react strongly to criticism or perceived threats to their self-image. Proverbs 15:1 (NIV) advises, "A gentle answer turns away wrath, but a harsh word stirs up anger."

- **Superficial Relationships:** Narcissists tend to form superficial relationships based on their own needs and desires. They may use people for personal gain and lack the ability to create deep emotional connections as long as they persist in a delusional state. 1 Corinthians 13:4-5 (NIV) emphasizes the importance of genuine love and selflessness in relationships: "Love is patient, love is kind. It does not envy, it does not boast, it is not proud."

- **Constant Need for Control:** Narcissists thrive on maintaining control in their relationships and often resist any challenges to their authority. They may disregard boundaries and seek to dominate others. In contrast,

Galatians 5:22-23 (NIV) highlights the fruit of the Spirit, which includes qualities like self-control: "But the fruit of the Spirit is love, joy, peace, forbearance, kindness, goodness, faithfulness, gentleness, and self-control."

Identifying a narcissist requires careful observation of these behavioral patterns and characteristics. It's essential to approach such situations with empathy and a desire to protect your well-being. Proverbs 4:23 (NIV) reminds us, "Above all else, guard your heart, for everything you do flows from it." By recognizing the signs of narcissism, you can make informed decisions about your relationships and interactions while keeping your heart guarded against potential harm.

2.1 Identifying a Narcissist: Signs and Spiritual Insight

When navigating the dating world, it's crucial to discern the signs and red flags that might indicate you are in the company of a narcissist. Narcissists possess a grandiose sense of self-importance and an insatiable need for attention and admiration. In your pursuit of a healthy and spiritually fulfilling relationship, here are some spiritual insights and red flags to help you identify a potential narcissist, complemented by relevant Bible verses.

- **Excessive Self-Centeredness:** Narcissists tend to dominate conversations with a focus on themselves and their achievements. They crave constant validation and may interrupt or dismiss others. In contrast, Philippians 2:3 (NIV) guides us to "do nothing out of selfish ambition or vain conceit. Rather, in humility, value others above yourselves."

- **Lack of Empathy:** A significant sign of narcissism is a lack of empathy, making it difficult for them to understand and relate to others' emotions. They may disregard your feelings. In contrast, 1 Peter 3:8 (NIV) encourages us to "be compassionate, be humble."

- **Manipulation and Control:** Narcissists often employ manipulative tactics, including gaslighting, to control situations and people to meet their needs. Such behavior contradicts Ephesians 4:29 (NIV): "Do not let any unwholesome talk come out of your mouths, but only what is helpful for building others up."

- **Lack of Boundaries:** Narcissists may disregard personal boundaries, infringing on your privacy and pressuring you. They may not respect your wishes and needs. Galatians 5:22-23 (NIV) reminds us of the importance of self-control and respecting the boundaries of others as part of the fruit of the Spirit.

- **Excessive Sense of Entitlement:** Narcissists believe they deserve special treatment and can become upset if their expectations are not met. In contrast, 1 Corinthians 10:24 (NIV) advises us: "No one should seek their own good, but the good of others."

Being spiritually attuned can help you recognize these signs and red flags when dating. A relationship built on humility, compassion, and mutual respect will likely be spiritually enriching and fulfilling. If you constantly encounter these narcissistic behaviors, this may indicate that you should seek guidance, support, or professional assistance, all while keeping in mind

Proverbs 4:23 (NIV): "Above all else, guard your heart, for everything you do flows from it.

2.2 Manipulation Tactics Employed by Narcissists: Recognizing the Signs

Narcissists are masters at concealing their true selves, especially in the early stages of a relationship. When it comes to dating, they are adept at putting on a charming facade, appearing loving, kind, and affectionate. However, it is essential to understand that this behavior is just an act. Behind the façade lies a manipulator who will do anything to get what they want.

Gaslighting: Distorting Reality

One manipulation tactic employed by narcissists is gaslighting. They subtly twist facts and manipulate situations to make their victim doubt their sanity and perception of reality. By sowing seeds of uncertainty, the narcissist gains control over the other person's thoughts and emotions, making them easier to manipulate. A person is like a bank account; in healthy relationships, people make emotional deposits daily in each other's accounts. A narcissist will refuse to make deposits. When you bring the situation to their attention, rather than meeting your relational needs, they tell you you're needy and that hugging, kissing, and other forms of intimacy are not normal behaviors. The victim starts to wonder if there is something wrong with them. Studies show that hugs and other forms of physical affection reduce stress, lower blood pressure, and have other health benefits; God made use so that we need each other to thrive.

Relevant Bible Verse:

2 Timothy 1:7 (NIV): "For the Spirit God gave us does not make us timid, but gives us power, love, and self-discipline."

Love Bombing: Intense But Fleeting Affection

Another tactic frequently used by narcissists is love bombing. In the early stages of a relationship, they shower their partner with excessive attention, compliments, and affection. This intense love and attention can make their target feel special and desired, creating a sense of dependency on the narcissist. However, once they have gained control over their victim, the love bombing quickly fades away. This deception tactic draws you into the trap, like the mouse who thought cheese was a gift.

Relevant Bible Verse:

Proverbs 27:6 (NIV): "Wounds from a friend can be trusted, but an enemy multiplies kisses."

Guilt Trips: Emotional Manipulation

Narcissists are also skilled at employing guilt trips to manipulate others. They will make their victim feel responsible for their unhappiness or failures, using emotional manipulation to elicit feelings of guilt and shame. Narcissists can easily bend their target's emotions to their will and maintain control over the relationship by playing on their target's emotions. A strange manipulation dynamic occurs within these types of relationships; the relationship becomes transactional instead of a God-ordained relational dynamic based on unconditional agape love. Whenever you do what the narcissist wants, they will shower you with affection, and if you do not do what they want, they will become cold and distant.

Relevant Bible Verse:

Psalm 32:5 (NIV): "Then I acknowledged my sin to you and did not cover up my iniquity. I said, 'I will confess my transgressions to the Lord.' And you forgave the guilt of my sin."

Isolation: Cutting Ties

Another tactic often utilized by narcissists is isolation. They will gradually distance their victim from friends and family, making them increasingly dependent on the narcissist for emotional support and validation. Through this isolation, the narcissist gains further control over their partner's thoughts, feelings, and actions, making it easier to manipulate them.

Relevant Bible Verse:

Proverbs 18:1 (NIV): "An unfriendly person pursues selfish ends and against all sound judgment starts quarrels."

Passive-Aggressive Behavior and Silent Treatment: Controlling Through Withdrawal

Narcissists excel at manipulating their victims through passive-aggressive behavior and the silent treatment. They will deliberately withhold affection, attention, or communication to punish their partner or gain control over a particular situation. This manipulation tactic can leave their victim feeling confused, desperate for attention, and willing to comply with the narcissist's demands.

Relevant Bible Verse:

Proverbs 15:1 (NIV): "A gentle answer turns away wrath, but a harsh word stirs up anger."

Narcissists possess a wide range of manipulative tactics, which they employ to get what they want. Their ability to hide their true selves and their skilled manipulation tactics make them formidable and dangerous individuals to be involved with. Recognizing these tactics is crucial in protecting oneself from falling prey to their manipulation and maintaining healthy relationships.

2.3 Real-Life Examples Illustrating Narcissistic Behaviors.

"Charles Spurgeon, a renowned English Christian preacher, once said, 'A good character, when established, is not easily overthrown by malignant toadstools (poisonous people). Even poisonous people can't destroy someone the Lord has graced character, but a character crusted with vices and rotten with corruption is soon demolished. It may appear beautiful on the surface for a little while, but it is at heart a ruin and soon falls with a crash.' This quote holds true when examining the behaviors of narcissists. One way to understand the nature of these individuals is to explore real-life examples and anecdotes that illustrate their actions and patterns of thought."

John Wesley and His Narcissistic Wife:

In the 18th century, John Wesley, the revered founder of the Methodist church, lived a life filled with immense dedication to God and reaching the lost. However, despite his profound impact on the spiritual landscape, he faced significant challenges in his personal life. His wife, who can be described as a narcissist, exerted an unrelenting grip on him, stopping at nothing to maintain control over his actions. Instances such as pulling him across the room by his hair and publicly mocking and lying about him were sadly not uncommon.

In the confines of their private life, John Wesley's wife employed various tactics to assert her dominance and manipulate him. It is heartbreaking to imagine the pain he endured as she physically exerted control over him by aggressively pulling him across the room by his hair. This act of physical cruelty displays a distressing level of power imbalance within their relationship, as John Wesley, a prominent figure, was subjected to such demeaning treatment.

The emotional abuse inflicted by his wife was equally damaging. In a disturbing revelation, her malicious intent is evident in her public mockery and lies about John Wesley. The public arena became a stage for her to demean and discredit him, painting a distorted image of his character. Such actions undermine his authority and aim to isolate and humiliate him, making it difficult for him to carry out God's calling and mission effectively.

Despite his immense hardships, John Wesley remained steadfast in his dedication to his beliefs and mission. His wife's efforts to control and hinder him were met with resilience and unwavering determination. He did not allow her narcissistic behavior to overshadow his work's importance; instead, he rose above adversity, striving to spread the gospel of Jesus Christ.

Wesley once sent an unflinching message demanding Molly be content and submit: 'Know me and know yourself, said Wesley. Suspect me no more, aspire (determine in your heart to attack or criticize my reputation or question my integrity) me no more, and provoke me no more: do no longer contend for mastery (stop trying to control me). Be content to be a private insignificant(a person of little reputation). A person, known and loved by God and me.'

It is disheartening to reflect on the extent to which John Wesley's wife went to obstruct his path. Her actions, driven by a narcissistic desire for control, serve as a stark reminder of the immense challenges and sacrifices he endured. Yet, his unwavering commitment to the Lord and the tremendous impact he had on the world through the preaching of the gospel stands as a testament to his remarkable strength, resilience, and faith in God.

John Wesley endured a turbulent marriage with a narcissistic wife who would stop at nothing to control and hinder him. From physically exerting her dominance by pulling him across the room by his hair to publicly mocking and lying about him, her actions were a profound reflection of her manipulative nature. However, despite facing such hardships, John Wesley remained steadfast in his commitment to the great commission and dedicated his life to spreading the gospel of Christ. His resilience when faced with adversity inspires generations, reminding us that even amid personal trials, one can honor the Lord.

Leadership and Narcissistic Tendencies:

In any organization, a typical leader wants their people to excel beyond their abilities. They recognize that by fostering growth and empowering their team members, the organization as a whole will thrive. However, some leaders possess narcissistic tendencies and are easily offended when their subordinates begin to surpass them. This is particularly evident in a scenario where a Narcissistic Pastor hires young ministers who, over time, start to excel in their roles beyond his gift.

At first, the Narcissistic Pastor may have hired these ministers, expecting they would support his vision and help him build a solid and thriving church community. However, as these young ministers begin to shine in their respective roles and demonstrate abilities that surpass the Pastor's talents, he starts to feel threatened. The selfish side of his personality takes over, and instead of celebrating their success, he becomes controlling and begins to undermine their accomplishments.

This control manifests itself in various ways. The Narcissistic Pastor may belittle their achievements, take credit for their ideas, or constantly nitpick their work. He may even attempt to sabotage them by assigning tasks beyond their capabilities or purposefully excluding them from important decisions. The Pastor's insecurities fuel his need for control, as seeing others excel beyond his abilities constantly reminds him of his limitations.

This situation mirrors the biblical story of David and Saul. Saul, who started as Israel's first king, initially embraced David and recognized his abilities. However, as David's fame and success grew, Saul became increasingly jealous and began to perceive him as a threat. He even attempted to kill him, fearing David would usurp his throne. In both the biblical story and the scenario of the young pastor, the fear of being overshadowed by those they have hired leads to insecurity and a desperate desire for control.

It is crucial to recognize and address these narcissistic tendencies within leadership. By fostering a culture of collaboration and celebrating the success of others, a leader can create an environment where individuals are encouraged to excel beyond their abilities. Doing so benefits the organization and enables each team member to reach their full potential. In this environment, the leader's weaknesses are compensated for by the strengths of others and vice versa.

The New Testament Saul:

Saul was a Pharisee, a religious leader in Israel, and well-known. The Pharisees tended to be very wealthy, well connected and loved to flaunt it. When we examine the actions and beliefs of the Pharisees and Saul in the New Testament, it becomes evident that their mentality aligns closely with narcissistic tendencies. They were preoccupied with status, power, and control; they constantly sought positions that would enable them to exert authority over others. Their pursuit of religious power was driven not by a genuine desire to make a positive impact or to bring people closer to God but rather to have dominion over them.

The Pharisees, known for their obsession with rules and regulations, created an elaborate framework of requirements and obligations God did not mandate. They delighted in making people follow these burdensome laws, placing heavy loads on their shoulders while failing to adhere to them. This hypocritical behavior exemplifies the narcissist's propensity for enforcing strict standards on others while exempting themselves from the same obligations.

Saul, later known as Paul, displayed narcissistic tendencies as well. Before his conversion, he actively persecuted early Christians and sought to eliminate any dissenting voices. His vigorous pursuit of power and control led him to believe that he was justified in his actions, disregarding the well-being and rights of others. Saul's transformation into Paul, later guided by humility and compassion, exemplifies the possibility of change and growth but also serves as a reminder of the narcissistic tendencies that initially drove him.

Recognizing these similarities between narcissistic behavior and the mindset of the Pharisees and Saul allows us to reflect on the importance of avoiding such distortions in our own lives. We must strive to be motivated by genuine empathy, compassion, and a desire to uplift others rather than seek power and control for our benefit. By developing self-awareness and focusing on the well-being of those around us, we can avoid falling into the trap of narcissism and contribute positively to the lives of others.

The transformation of Saul into Paul is a powerful testimony to the life-changing power of the Lord. In Acts 9:1-19, we witness the extraordinary events that unfolded on the road to Damascus. Blinded by his narcissistic tendencies, Saul was confronted by a divine intervention that shook him to his core.

While Saul was on this road, with intentions to persecute Christians, the Lord appeared to him in a blinding light. Saul was knocked off his horse and humbled by the presence of God. At that moment, Saul's arrogance and self-righteousness were shattered, and he realized the error of his ways.

From that point forward, Saul's life was forever changed. He underwent a miraculous conversion and became one of the most influential figures in spreading the teachings of Christianity. His inner transformation was so profound that he even took on a new name, Paul, symbolizing humility.

This account serves as a testament to the fact that people can change. Indeed, we should never enter into relationships or interactions with the expectation of changing someone else.

However, it is crucial to recognize that people can undergo transformative growth through divine intervention, personal reflection, or profound life experiences.

Paul's story shows us that even those deeply entrenched in their own misguided beliefs and destructive behaviors can be redeemed. It encourages those who doubt their ability to change or question whether others can.

Remember that change may not always come quickly or without some intervention. Sometimes, a significant event compels individuals to reevaluate their actions and beliefs. However, Saul's transformation into Paul teaches us that change is possible with the right circumstances and the grace of God.

When you hear people say that people can't change, share with them the account of Saul's transformation into Paul. Help them understand that while change may require a profound shift in perspective, it is within the realm of possibility for everyone.

These real-life examples illustrate narcissists' complex and often destructive behaviors in various contexts, from personal relationships to leadership and religious positions. They serve as cautionary tales and reminders of the importance of recognizing and addressing narcissistic tendencies in ourselves and others and seeking positive change when needed.

2.4 Effects of Narcissism on Others (Galatians 5:19-21)

With its inherent self-centeredness, narcissism carries consequences for those in its orbit. Galatians 5:19-21 offers a spiritual perspective on the effects of such behavior: "The acts of the flesh are obvious: sexual immorality, impurity, and debauchery; idolatry and witchcraft; hatred, discord, jealousy, fits of rage, selfish ambition, dissensions, factions, and envy; drunkenness, orgies, and the like. As I did before, I warn you that those who live like this will not inherit the kingdom of God." (Galatians 5:19-21, NIV)

While this verse primarily addresses broader sinful behaviors, it underscores the destructive nature of self-centeredness and the relational turmoil it can create. It's also essential to remember that Greek and Roman cultures were influential worldwide when these verses were written, and many narcissistic behaviors were celebrated. If the early church could walk away from these behaviors in these environments, it's possible in any cultural setting.

Narcissistic behavior often leads to:

- **Emotional Turmoil:** Those in relationships with narcissists frequently experience emotional turmoil, including feelings of neglect, frustration, and emotional exhaustion. Narcissists' constant need for admiration and validation can leave loved ones feeling drained and unappreciated.

- **Conflict and Discord:** Narcissistic individuals may engage in manipulative behaviors, causing discord and conflict within relationships. Their inability to empathize or take responsibility for their actions can lead to ongoing strife.

- **Damaged Self-Esteem:** Those close to narcissists may suffer from diminished self-esteem and worth due to constant criticism or a sense of being overshadowed by the narcissist's ego.

- **Isolation:** Narcissists may isolate their loved ones, distancing them from friends and family to maintain control over the relationship.

- **Lack of Authentic Connection:** Authenticity and vulnerability, essential for deep, meaningful connections, often suffer in relationships with narcissists. Their focus on self-image and self-preservation inhibits genuine intimacy.

Galatians 5:19-21 serves as a reminder of the consequences of self-centered behavior. While not explicitly addressing narcissism, it underscores the destructive impact of actions rooted in self-indulgence and self-interest. Those who engage in such conduct, as well as those affected by them, may find themselves distanced from the qualities that align with the kingdom of God, including love, joy, peace, patience, kindness, goodness, faithfulness, gentleness, and self-control (Galatians 5:22-23).

Recognizing The effect of narcissism on others is vital to understanding the need for healing and transformation. It highlights the importance of breaking free from the cycle of self-centeredness, embracing vulnerability, and cultivating relationships marked by authenticity, compassion, and a deeper connection with God and those around us.

CHAPTER THREE
NAVIGATING RELATIONSHIPS
WITH NARCISSISTS

Navigating relationships with narcissists can be incredibly challenging, requiring a delicate balance of wisdom, patience, and understanding rooted in biblical principles. As discussed earlier, these individuals often possess traits such as an inflated sense of self-importance, a constant need for admiration, and a lack of empathy for others.

It's crucial to set clear boundaries and maintain self-respect, as Proverbs 4:23 (NIV) advised: "Above all else, guard your heart, for everything you do flows from it." These emotional and interpersonal boundaries will help protect your well-being and prevent manipulation.

Decisions, Decisions

Narcissism is defined as 'an excessive interest in or admiration of oneself and one's physical appearance.' Narcissists are known for their self-centeredness and lack of empathy, which can manifest in many ways. One of these ways is their tendency to attempt to take away an individual's decision-making ability. This will explore narcissists' tactics to take away an individual's ability to make decisions and the psychological impacts of such behavior.

Narcissists often attempt to control a person's decision-making ability through manipulation and coercion. For example, they might try to intimidate the person into making certain decisions by threatening or using guilt tactics. They may also use gaslighting to make the individual doubt themselves and their choices or use excessive flattery to influence the person's decisions. Additionally, they may attempt to control the person's environment, limiting their access to resources or people that could help them make decisions.

These tactics are used to undermine an individual's sense of autonomy and self-determination. When a person is deprived of the ability to make their own decisions, it can have a profound psychological impact. This can lead to feelings of helplessness, worthlessness, and even depression. It can also lead to a lack of self-confidence and trust in your own judgment and a fear of making decisions and taking responsibility.

Furthermore, when a person is not allowed to make their own decisions, it can lead to a lack of motivation and a feeling of being trapped and unable to move forward. This can lead to a decrease in productivity, as well as a decrease in their sense of satisfaction and accomplishment. Additionally, it can lead to resentment and anger towards the narcissist, which may eventually manifest as a feeling of helplessness and hopelessness.

While narcissists may struggle with empathy, practicing compassion and understanding aligns with our Christian values. Romans 12:15 (NIV) reminds us to "Rejoice with those who rejoice; mourn with those who mourn." Empathizing with their struggles while avoiding enabling destructive behavior is critical.

Support Groups

Engage with a support network and seek wise counsel from trusted friends, family members, or a counselor, following the guidance of Proverbs 11:14 (NIV): "For lack of guidance a nation falls, but victory is won through many advisers." Such a supportive community can provide insight and emotional strength.

If you are looking for counseling, many church groups, support groups, and organizations can provide you with the help you need. These groups are especially helpful if you feel you cannot afford professional counseling or cannot access it. Church groups can provide spiritual guidance and emotional support. Support groups are often led by lay people who have experienced similar issues or struggles and are willing to share their experiences and offer help. In addition, many organizations, such as Alcoholics Anonymous, Narcotics Anonymous, and other addiction support groups, provide counseling services for those struggling with addiction. No matter what type of counseling you need, these groups will provide a safe, non-judgmental atmosphere to discuss your struggles and find the help you need.

Expectations

Maintain realistic expectations in your interactions with narcissists, understanding that they may not change quickly, if at all. Philippians 4:6 (NIV) encourages us: "Do not be anxious about anything, but in every situation, by prayer and petition, with thanksgiving, present your requests to God." Pray for wisdom and guidance while embracing that you cannot fundamentally alter their personality. This said, trusting the Lord for the best outcome is still essential.

Prioritize self-care to safeguard your emotional and mental well-being, in line with Galatians 6:4-5 (NIV): "Each one should test their own actions. Then they can take pride in themselves alone, without comparing themselves to someone else, for each one should carry their own load." Focus on self-improvement and growth, irrespective of the narcissist's actions.

Lastly, maintain a strong foundation in your faith. Psalm 46:1 (NIV) offers comfort: "God is our refuge and strength, an ever-present help in trouble." Your faith can provide the strength and resilience to navigate these challenging relationships.

3.1 Discuss strategies to protect yourself from falling into a relationship with a narcissist.

Guarding your heart is an essential biblical principle that is particularly crucial when safeguarding yourself from entering a relationship with a narcissist. As Proverbs 4:23 (NIV) advises, "Above all else, guard your heart, for everything you do flows from it." This scripture underscores the need for caution and discernment when selecting marital or relational partners. If you are someone who is affectionate and likes to help people, you have to be even more cautious when choosing a mate because you tend to want to help hurting people, and if you are looking for a mate, you should not be looking for someone who needs your help and is hurting. What you should be looking for when contemplating marriage is someone who is emotionally and spiritually mature and already serving in the church as a single person. The Bible highlights the importance of being selective and vigilant in your choices.

One strategy to protect yourself from entangling with a narcissist is to exercise discernment. When seeking long-term relationships, remember that being selective is a positive trait. It enables you to evaluate potential partners based on their character, values, and treatment of others. Take your time to get to know them before committing emotionally, and heed any red flags that may signal narcissistic tendencies.

Open communication, a cornerstone of healthy relationships, is pivotal in guarding against narcissists. An effective strategy is to express your needs and boundaries clearly from the outset, as recommended in Ephesians 4:15 (NIV): "Instead, speaking the truth in love, we will grow to become in every respect the mature body of him who is the head, that is, Christ." Narcissists often push boundaries and manipulate situations to suit their desires. By articulating your limits, you make it easier to recognize when someone attempts to exploit or control you for their benefit.

Self-awareness plays a crucial role in safeguarding yourself from a narcissistic partner. Take time to reflect on your vulnerabilities and past relationship patterns. This introspection enables you to identify any inclinations to be attracted to or attract selfish individuals. By being conscious of your tendencies, you can intentionally make healthier choices and avoid falling into familiar patterns.

Seeking support from trusted friends and family aligns with the biblical principle of Proverbs 11:14 (NIV): "For lack of guidance, a nation falls, but victory is won through many advisers." Narcissists excel at manipulation and can make you doubt your judgment. A robust support system, offering guidance and feedback, is invaluable in helping you see the truth of a situation and steer clear of a relationship with a narcissist.

Guarding your heart, rooted in biblical wisdom, holds profound significance in protecting yourself from involvement with a narcissist. Practicing selectivity, maintaining clear communication of boundaries, fostering self-awareness, and seeking support all contribute to avoiding harmful and manipulative relationships. Remember that it is wiser to exercise caution and discernment in selecting a partner than to become trapped in a relationship that inflicts emotional distress and harm.

3.2 Tips on setting boundaries and recognizing manipulation techniques.

When navigating a relationship with a narcissist, it's vital to establish and maintain healthy boundaries while recognizing manipulation techniques. Proverbs 25:28 (NIV) wisely states, "Like a city whose walls are broken through is a person who lacks self-control." Just as a city's walls protect its inhabitants, boundaries safeguard your emotional well-being and self-esteem.

One essential tip for setting boundaries with a narcissistic partner is to assert your autonomy. Narcissists often seek control in various aspects of the relationship, as Proverbs 21:9 (NIV) mentioned: "Better to live on a corner of the roof than share a house with a quarrelsome wife." To assert your autonomy, express your preferences and opinions confidently. If they consistently dismiss your choices or try to manipulate you into changing your mind, it's a clear sign that they do not respect your boundaries.

Recognizing manipulation techniques is crucial. Narcissists may employ tactics such as guilt-tripping, gaslighting, or emotional manipulation, as warned against in Proverbs 6:16-19 (NIV): "There are six things the Lord hates, seven that are detestable to him: haughty eyes, a lying tongue, hands that shed innocent blood, a heart that devises wicked schemes, feet that are quick to rush into evil, a false witness who pours out lies and a person who stirs up conflict in the community." Trust your instincts and be vigilant when you notice attempts to undermine your self-confidence or judgment.

Observing their reactions when you assert your boundaries provides valuable insights into their true nature. A narcissist will likely respond with anger, defensiveness, or dismissiveness when faced with newly established limits. They may even attempt to reverse the situation and portray you as unreasonable. It's important to recognize this behavior as a manipulation technique and remain resolute in maintaining your boundaries.

Remember that you deserve to be in a healthy and mutually respectful relationship. Philippians 2:3-4 (NIV) advises, "Do nothing out of selfish ambition or vain conceit. Rather, in humility, value others above yourselves, not looking to your own interests but each of you to the interests of the others." If you consistently experience emotional drain or disrespect, it may be time to contemplate ending the relationship for your well-being. Seek professional assistance or confide in a trusted individual who can offer support during this process.

Setting and maintaining boundaries while recognizing manipulation techniques is essential when dealing with a narcissistic partner. Just as a city's walls protect its residents, your boundaries safeguard your emotional health. By asserting your autonomy, identifying manipulation tactics, and trusting your instincts, you can preserve your well-being and seek the healthy, respectful relationship you deserve.

3.3 The importance of self-care and maintaining one's emotional well-being.

Meeting emotional needs and maintaining well-being are crucial aspects of a fulfilling life. While our relationships with family and others can play a significant role in meeting these needs, it's equally essential to recognize the importance of self-care and personal responsibility. Developing a deep intimacy with God and learning contentment can be powerful aids on this journey.

Self-care entails deliberately nurturing our physical, mental, and emotional selves. It involves prioritizing activities that uplift our spirits, bring us joy, and grant us inner peace. Engaging in rest, pursuing hobbies, exercising and meditating on God's word, and seeking professional assistance when necessary are all ways to ensure our emotional needs are met healthily and sustainably. Self-care also fosters self-awareness, empowering us to understand better and manage our emotions.

While our relationships contribute significantly to our emotional well-being, it's unrealistic and burdensome to place the entire responsibility on others. People have limitations, and relying solely on external sources for emotional support can lead to dependency and strain on these relationships. By embracing self-care practices, we take ownership of our emotional states and actively work towards nurturing our well-being.

Developing a deep intimacy with God is another transformative element in maintaining emotional well-being. Walking in the Spirit, fulfilling the great commission, and living a life of faith provides a profound sense of purpose, guidance, and comfort, even during adversity. Individuals can find strength and comfort by cultivating a close relationship with the Lord, allowing them to navigate life's trials with resilience and peace.

Learning the art of contentment is equally vital for emotional well-being. Contentment involves accepting ourselves and our life circumstances and finding fulfillment in the present moment. It liberates us from constantly pursuing external validation or the need to compare ourselves to others. Cultivating contentment reduces stress and enables us to focus on nurturing our emotional health, leading to a happier and more fulfilling life.

While our emotional needs find fulfillment through relationships, practicing self-care and taking personal responsibility for our emotional well-being are essential. By deepening our relationship with God, embracing contentment, and engaging in activities that promote joy and inner peace, we ensure that our emotional needs are met in a healthy and sustainable way. Taking charge of our emotional lives is vital for personal growth, nurturing healthy relationships, and experiencing overall well-being.

Walking In The Spirit

The bible says walk in the Spirit and you will not fulfill the lusts of the flesh, selfishness is a lust of the flesh and a work of the flesh and walking in the Spirit by practicing these Spiritual disciplines will set you free. Praying in the Spirit, reading the Word, and worshiping God are some of the most important and effective spiritual disciplines for Christians. When practiced regularly, these activities can open us up to the glory and presence of God.

Praying in the Spirit can be a powerful and transformative experience. Praying in the Spirit involves praying in a language that is not your own but a heavenly language that only God can understand. It is a way of praying that allows us to bypass our own limited understanding and commune with God on a deeper level. Praying in the Spirit helps us to gain greater clarity and understanding of God's will and plan for our lives.

God has given us these spiritual disciplines that can help keep us grounded and healthy, emotionally, mentally, and otherwise, and this starts with reading the word. Reading the Word of God is an essential spiritual discipline. The Bible is God's Word, and it can be a source of life and guidance for us. Studying and meditating on God's Word helps us to understand His character and ways, as well as His promises and commands. When we read the Bible regularly, we gain a greater understanding of God and His plan for us.

Finally, worshiping God is an important spiritual discipline. Worship is a way of expressing our love and adoration for God. It is a way of acknowledging Him as Lord and Savior and expressing our gratitude for all that He has done for us. Worshiping God can open us up to His presence and deepen our relationship with Him.

When we engage in these spiritual disciplines regularly, we can access the glory of God. I have personally experienced this in my own prayer closet. I have gone in discouraged and come out so high in the Spirit that I forgot why I was discouraged.

These spiritual disciplines are important for Christians to practice if we want to grow in our faith and deepen our relationship with God. Praying in the Spirit, reading the Word, and worshipping God are powerful spiritual disciplines that can open us up to the glory and majesty of God.

CHAPTER FOUR

THE POWER OF VULNERABILITY:
A DIVINE STRENGTH (2 CORINTHIANS 12:9)

In the pursuit of overcoming narcissism and cultivating authentic connections, the concept of vulnerability stands as a divine strength, beautifully exemplified in 2 Corinthians 12:9: "But he said to me, 'My grace is sufficient for you, for my power is made perfect in weakness.' Therefore, I will boast all the more gladly of my weaknesses so that the power of Christ may rest upon me." (2 Corinthians 12:9, ESV)

This verse from the Apostle Paul's letter to the Corinthians underscores the divine truth that God's power shines most brilliantly through our vulnerabilities and weaknesses. It offers a transformative perspective on embracing vulnerability as a conduit for experiencing God's grace and strength in our lives.

Proverbs 28:13: "If you hide your sins, you will not succeed. If you confess and reject them, you will receive mercy."

Psalm 69:5: "God, you know what I have done wrong; I cannot hide my guilt from you."

Psalm 44:20-21 "If we had forgotten the name of our God or lifted our hands to a foreign god, wouldn't God find out since he knows the secrets of the heart?"

Psalm 90:8: "You have set our wrong-doing before You, our secret sins in the light of Your face."

In all these scriptures, the message is that if you show me your real heart, sins, and all, I will embrace, love, and show you mercy. When we expose our weaknesses and make ourselves vulnerable, grace comes on us; he gives grace to the humble; grace is unmerited favor and the ability to do a thing. The first step we take towards humility is transparency. The book's title is Unlocking the Strength of Vulnerability to Conquer Narcissism. A relationship is based on honesty and transparency. A phrase they use in our day is I see you. It means you are important to me; you will not be overlooked. God sees all of his children like a parent who watches a child playing on the playground;

Even though parents love watching their kids play on the playground, watching and protecting them from afar is not a substitute for the relational intimacy of sharing, hugs, and kisses, hurts, wounds, and successes — allowing thim to see the true you, sins, failures, successes, fears, everything. This principle holds true in our relationship with the Lord. He considers all and knows all, yet he still desires an intimate relationship with us. This is a Revelation that, when it is embraced, should cause you to take the locks off the doors of your heart, swing open the door of your being, and ask the Lord to move in, Lord make me a habitation, sanctify me, let my heart be your holiest place. Let my heart be your hiding place, and let me rest in your presence. When we tell the Lord the truth about who we are and where we are, it's not only making things right with God confessing our sins, but it's our daily opportunity to be naked and unafraid, like Adam and Eve in the garden, they were free (because of their divine connection with God they could shout every day someone knows and loves me for who I am), their heart and soul their everything, they walked with God hand in hand. When they disobeyed God, they hid themselves and lost their intimacy and vulnerability; there was now a wall between man and God because of sin, a wall of sin and shame. God is Holy; he cannot fellowship with evil, so paradise was lost. Jesus died on the cross to restore that intimacy; now you can come to God as they did in the garden naked and unafraid (vulnerable) through Christ. Repent and Surrender your heart in faith to Jesus; he will forgive your sins, removing the wall that separates you from mercy and grace. Now, you can live authentically and vulnerably in his presence, loved unconditionally. You don't have to perform for him; he loves you unconditionally, and he loves you before you do anything. We obey him to express our love, not to get his love.

Vulnerability as Authenticity:

Vulnerability is rooted in authenticity — being open and honest about our true selves, including our flaws and imperfections. By embracing our vulnerabilities, we create space for genuine connections with others and with God.

Overcoming Narcissism:

Narcissism often thrives on the fear of being vulnerable. It stems from a desire to protect one's self-image at all costs. However, 2 Corinthians 12:9 encourages us to let go of this fear, recognizing that it is in our weaknesses that God's power is most evident.

Divine Grace in Vulnerability:

Embracing vulnerability is an act of trust in God's grace. It involves surrendering our pride and self-sufficiency acknowledging that we need His strength to navigate life's challenges. The Old-time revivalists used to call Jesus the great physician. If you go to the surgeon, does he allow or need you to help him to operate? No, he will not, and he does not. All the surgeon requires you to do is take your medicine(the word and prayer), lay down on the table, and allow him to operate. It takes faith to lay on that table; you have to believe in the skillfulness of the surgeon. Jesus has never lost a patient, and his skill is unmatched in all the universe; right now, put your heart in his hands. Tell him, Lord, I am yours.

Authentic Connections:

Vulnerability fosters authentic connections with others, allowing us to be truly seen and understood. It serves as the bridge to overcoming the isolating effects of narcissism and building meaningful relationships. The cause of this fear of vulnerability is rooted in pride and a fear of being rejected. We naturally want to present the best version of ourselves to the world, to appear strong and capable. But this is a false sense of security because it keeps us from experiencing the true depths of relationships. We fear we will be rejected and judged if we reveal our true selves, flaws, and vulnerabilities. But this is far from the truth; if you throw yourself out there and allow yourself to be vulnerable, you will find that most people appreciate authenticity. They will see your courage and will be drawn to you for it. Your refusal to be vulnerable is preventing you from creating meaningful connections and forming strong and lasting relationships. You are self-sabotaging, creating a self-fulfilling prophecy that will only lead to further loneliness and isolation. But this doesn't have to be the case. It's time to take a leap of faith and open yourself up to the world, you will be surprised by the love and acceptance that comes your way.

God's Strength Manifested:

As we allow ourselves to be vulnerable, we position ourselves to experience the transformative power of God's strength in our lives.

His grace fills the void our weaknesses create, enabling us to navigate life's trials with resilience and faith.

Biblical wisdom is that vulnerability is not a weakness but a pathway to the Lord's strength. It encourages readers to embrace their vulnerabilities, let go of the fear of being exposed, and experience the grace and power of Christ in their journey to overcome narcissism and cultivate authentic, spiritually enriched connections.

4.1 Vulnerability as a Divine Virtue

Vulnerability emerges as a divine virtue rooted in Christ-like humility and authenticity when viewed through a spiritual lens. It is a quality that aligns with the principles of selflessness, compassion, and genuine connection advocated in the Bible.

Christ's Example of Vulnerability:

The life of Jesus Christ serves as the ultimate example of vulnerability. His willingness to become human, experience suffering, and offer Himself as a sacrifice for humanity demonstrates the divine strength found in vulnerability.

"In your relationships with one another, have the same mindset as Christ Jesus: Who, being in very nature God, did not consider equality with God something to be used to his advantage; rather, he made himself nothing by taking the very nature of a servant, being made in human likeness." (Philippians 2:5-7, NIV)

Humility and Authenticity:

Vulnerability requires humility, willingness to acknowledge our limitations, imperfections, and need for God's grace. It involves authenticity, allowing others to see our true selves, both strengths and weaknesses. "Humble yourselves, therefore, under the mighty hand of God so that at the proper time he may exalt you." (1 Peter 5:6, ESV)

Fostering Genuine Connections:

Vulnerability is the key to fostering genuine, meaningful connections with others. It opens the door to empathy, compassion, and the ability to honestly understand and support one another. "Bear one another's burdens, and so fulfill the law of Christ." (Galatians 6:2, ESV)

Strength in Weakness:

Embracing vulnerability is an acknowledgment that our true strength lies in our weakness, as God's power is made perfect in our moments of vulnerability. "But he said to me, 'My grace is sufficient for you, for my power is made perfect in weakness.'" (2 Corinthians 12:9, ESV)

Incorporating the concept of vulnerability as a divine strength encourages readers to see vulnerability not as a weakness to be feared but as a strength to be cultivated, unlock it in your life, and open your heart. It invites them to follow the example of Christ, embracing humility, authenticity, and genuine connection as they seek to overcome narcissism and align their lives with the principles of spiritual growth and transformation.

The apostle Paul endured almost every conceivable hardship, yet he still thrived. His success was not based on his strength or abilities but on his reliance on God. He was never ashamed of his weaknesses but instead was proud of them, knowing that God would use them to bring about His will. Paul knew that the God he served was so powerful that He could use any circumstance to bring about His will for good. Despite the difficulties, the apostle Paul was a success because of his reliance and trust in God. His faith enabled him to endure and thrive despite the hardships he faced. He knew that he was weak and that God was strong, and this trust in the Lord gave him the strength and courage to face whatever challenges he encountered. In the end, Paul's faith in God was the key factor in his success.

4.2 Compassion for Victims of Narcissism (Psalm 34:18)

In the journey to overcome narcissism and foster authentic connections, it's crucial to emphasize the significance of compassion for those who have been affected by narcissistic behavior. Psalm 34:18 beautifully captures the essence of this compassion:

"The LORD is close to the brokenhearted and saves those who are crushed in spirit." (Psalm 34:18, NIV) This verse reassures us of God's presence and comfort for those who have suffered from narcissism's effects,

Highlighting the importance of extending compassion to them.

Acknowledging Their Pain:

Compassion begins with acknowledging the pain and suffering victims of narcissism have endured. It involves listening without judgment and providing a safe space for them to express their emotions. Active listening is listening to understand rather than to interpret and respond.

Offering Support and Validation:

Victims of narcissism often struggle with self-esteem issues and self-doubt. Compassion involves offering support and validation, helping them rebuild their self-worth and regain confidence.

Embracing Vulnerability in Healing:

Compassion encourages victims to embrace vulnerability in their healing journey. It invites them to explore their emotions and experiences without fear, fostering a sense of authenticity and self-discovery.

Reflecting God's Love:

As we extend compassion to victims of narcissism, we reflect God's love and grace. We become instruments of His comfort and healing, mirroring His care for the brokenhearted. People who have been hurt in relationships need Agape love, that unconditional love they receive freely, without having to perform or be perfect. This kind of love is what they often need the most, something they can rely on and trust, regardless of the situation or their feelings. Agape love is the kind of love that sees beyond a person's imperfections and instead sees the best in them. It is the kind of love that loves them unconditionally, no matter what they have done or said. This type of love gives them the confidence to move forward and try again, knowing someone loves them no matter what. It is the kind of love that helps them to forgive and to be able to receive love again. Agape love is the kind of love that gives them the strength to never give up, even in the face of adversity. It is the kind of love that helps them to realize their worth, and that they are worthy of being loved. Agape love is the kind of love that gives them the courage to love again, and to never give up on themselves or their dreams.

Encouraging Forgiveness and Wholeness:

Compassion plays a pivotal role in guiding victims toward forgiveness and wholeness. It helps them release the burden of resentment and find inner peace.

Nurturing Authentic Connections:

Compassion is a powerful force that helps us to understand and connect with others who have experienced the pain of narcissism. It helps us to open up and share our experiences, allowing us to offer support and understanding to those who are also healing. Compassion allows us to recognize our shared experience of pain and to form authentic connections with others who have experienced the same. Through compassion, we can lend an ear to listen, a shoulder to cry on, and a hand to help. It is a powerful tool that fosters deep understanding and connection between individuals as we recognize our similarities and support each other as we all work to heal. Compassion creates an environment of empathy, understanding, and mutual support, creating bonds that will last a lifetime.

Aligning with Biblical Principles:

Compassion aligns with the biblical principles of love and empathy emphasized throughout the Bible. It exemplifies the call to love our neighbors as ourselves (Matthew 22:36-40) and to comfort those in need.

4.3 Vulnerability as a Bridge to Grace

Vulnerability, when embraced with humility and authenticity, serves as a bridge to the grace of God. It is a transformative journey that allows individuals to experience God's unmerited favor and love in their lives.

Acknowledging Imperfections:

Vulnerability begins with acknowledging our imperfections and limitations. It is an admission that we are not perfect and that we need God's grace to navigate life's challenges.

"But he said to me, 'My grace is sufficient for you, for my power is made perfect in weakness.' Therefore, I will boast all the more gladly about my weaknesses, so that Christ's power may rest on me." (2 Corinthians 12:9, NIV)

A Surrender to God's Will:

Embracing vulnerability is an act of surrender to God's will. It involves letting go of the need to control and allowing God to work in and through our weaknesses.

"Trust in the LORD with all your heart, and do not lean on your own understanding. In all your ways acknowledge him, and he will make straight your paths." (Proverbs 3:5-6, ESV)

Encountering God's Unconditional Love:

As we open ourselves up to vulnerability, we encounter the depth of God's unconditional love and acceptance. His grace covers our shortcomings and offers us the assurance of His unwavering presence.

"But God, being rich in mercy, because of the great love with which he loved us, even when we were dead in our trespasses, made us alive together with Christ—by grace you have been saved." (Ephesians 2:4-5, ESV)

A Path to Redemption:

Vulnerability serves as a path to redemption. It allows individuals to confront their past mistakes, seek forgiveness, and experience the transformative power of God's grace in their lives. "Create in me a clean heart, O God, and renew a right spirit within me." (Psalm 51:10, ESV)

Vulnerability is often seen as a sign of weakness, but it can be a powerful path to redemption. When we open up and allow ourselves to be vulnerable, we can confront the mistakes we have made in our past and seek forgiveness. This process of self-reflection and accountability can be incredibly difficult, but it is essential in order for us to experience the transformative power of God's grace in our lives. We are reminded in Psalm 51:10 of God's loving mercy and grace, and that He is capable of renewing our spirits and creating in us a clean heart. Through vulnerability, we are able to open ourselves up to the transforming power of God's grace so that we may be redeemed and live a life of joy and peace.

A Source of Strength:

Vulnerability becomes a source of strength. It enables individuals to draw closer to God, develop resilience, and find comfort in His presence, even in the face of life's challenges.

CHAPTER FIVE
HELPING NARCISSISTS RECOVER

Helping narcissists recover can be challenging and complex, but it is not without hope. It's essential to approach this process with empathy, patience, and a deep understanding of the underlying issues. Here, we'll explore ways to assist narcissists in their journey toward recovery, all while drawing wisdom and guidance from the Bible.

- **Encourage Self-Reflection and Accountability:** Recovery often begins with self-awareness. Encourage the narcissist to reflect on their behaviors and their impact on themselves and others. In the Bible, 2 Corinthians 13:5 (NIV) says, "Examine yourselves to see whether you are in the faith; test yourselves. Do you not realize that Christ Jesus is in you unless, of course, you fail the test?" This verse emphasizes the importance of introspection and self-examination.

- **Offer Unconditional Love:** Loving a narcissist through their recovery process can be challenging but crucial. Proverbs 10:12 (NIV) reminds us, "Hatred stirs up conflict, but love covers over all wrongs." Your unwavering love and support can provide the emotional safety they need to confront their issues.

- **Encourage Professional Help:** Narcissism often requires professional intervention. Suggest therapy or counseling with a qualified mental health expert specializing in personality disorders, a Christian counselor, or a Pastor. Proverbs 15:22 (NIV) advises, "Plans fail for lack of counsel, but with many advisers, they succeed." Seek counsel from those who are equipped to address these complex issues.

- **Model Healthy Relationships:** Lead by example in demonstrating healthy, loving relationships. Show them the value of empathy, compassion, and humility. Philippians 2:3-4 (NIV) says, "Do nothing out of selfish ambition or vain conceit. Rather, in humility, value others above yourselves, not looking to your interests but each of you to the interests of the others."

- **Set Boundaries:** Establish clear boundaries to protect yourself from potential harm while showing love and support. Ephesians 4:2 (NIV) advises, "Be completely humble and gentle; be patient, bearing with one another in love." Balancing love and boundaries can be challenging but necessary.

- **Foster Spiritual Growth:** Encourage the narcissist to explore their faith and spirituality. Help them connect with their spiritual beliefs to find inner healing. Psalm 34:18 (NIV) reminds us, "The Lord is close to the brokenhearted and saves those who are crushed in spirit."

- **Practice Patience:** Recovery is often a slow and nonlinear process. Be patient and understanding, just as God is patient with us. Romans 15:1 (NIV) states, "We who are strong ought to bear with the failings of the weak and not to please ourselves."

- **Celebrate Progress:** Acknowledge and celebrate even small steps of progress. Luke 15:10 (NIV) reminds us, "In the same way, I tell you, there is rejoicing in the presence of the angels of God over one sinner who repents." Every positive change is a step closer to healing.

- **Pray for Guidance:** Seek divine guidance and wisdom through prayer. James 1:5 (NIV) assures us, "If any of you lacks wisdom, you should ask God, who gives generously to all without finding fault, and it will be given to you." Pray for discernment and direction in your efforts to help.

- **Deliverance and Counseling:** Deliverance and counseling are two different paths to freedom from addiction. Counseling is a process of learning about the root cause of the problem and working through it step by step with God's help until the person is slowly set free. On the other hand, deliverance is a supernatural act of God that instantly sets someone free. I had a friend who had been through counseling, and nothing had worked, but when they went to a deliverance service, they were instantly set free. It's important to remember that God knows best and to go the route He wants you to go. He may want you to go through counseling, or He may want to use deliverance to set you free. Either way, it is possible to be free from addiction and experience lasting freedom.

Assisting narcissists in their recovery is a challenging yet compassionate endeavor. Drawing wisdom from the Bible, we can approach this journey with love, patience, and faith. Through self-reflection, professional help, and unwavering support, there is hope for transformation and healing. Remember the words of Proverbs 11:25 (NIV), "A generous person will prosper; whoever refreshes others will be refreshed." Your efforts to help can lead to healing and transformation, benefiting both the narcissist and those around them.

5.1 Explore the potential for change and recovery in a narcissist.

Humility and brokenness are often considered the essential foundations for change and recovery in individuals, including narcissists. A prime example of this transformation can be witnessed in the story of King Nebuchadnezzar from the book of Daniel. His journey towards change commenced when his pride was shattered, and he surrendered himself to God's will.

In the book of Daniel, chapter 4 verse 34, it is written, "At the end of that time, I, Nebuchadnezzar, raised my eyes toward heaven, and my sanity was restored. Then I praised the Most High; I honored and glorified Him who lives forever." This verse highlights a crucial turning point in the life of King Nebuchadnezzar, where he acknowledges his submission to God and begins to reshape his perspective.

Narcissists often resist recognizing their faults or weaknesses. However, when these individuals experience a significant life event or personal crisis, such as King Nebuchadnezzar's loss of sanity, it can lead to a moment of vulnerability and self-reflection. This recognition creates an opportunity for change and recovery.

The critical factor in the transformation of a narcissist is their willingness to surrender their own will and embrace the Lord's plan for their lives. Through this surrender, narcissists can gain a fresh perspective on their behavior and its impact on themselves and those around them. It allows them to recognize the need for empathy, compassion, and humility, qualities that are often lacking in narcissistic personalities.

By embracing humility and brokenness, narcissists can embark on a path of self-improvement and healing. This process involves acknowledging their past behavior, making amends for any harm caused, and actively working towards growth and change. It requires a commitment to self-reflection, therapy, and personal development to overcome profoundly ingrained behavior and thought patterns. One of the reasons God gave us the bible was to renovate our minds. When someone renovates their home, they demolish it first and then bring in the new. The Bible does the same thing to our brains. But it won't happen with casual reading; you must dive deep to change. I GOT DEPLOYED TO THE DESERT when I gave my life to Christ. I was a corpsman in the Navy. The guy who helped me come to the Lord told me, you need to read your bible. Well, I took that statement literally. I read that bible from cover to cover three times, and when I came back, I was a changed man; I was full of joy, I didn't want to do the things I used to do, I was a new man, I wanted to talk about Jesus, I was changed from the inside out. You have to read the bible like you are looking for you. I applied every scripture to my life; if I was convicted, I repented.

While change and recovery in narcissists are undoubtedly challenging, the potential for transformation exists when they embrace humility and brokenness. Just as King Nebuchadnezzar's surrender to God's will restored his sanity, so too can narcissists find restoration by relinquishing their self-centeredness and embracing a new perspective focused on personal growth, empathy, and genuine connection with others.

James 4:10 (NIV) - "Humble yourselves before the Lord, and he will lift you up."

1 Peter 5:6 (NIV) - "Humble yourselves, therefore, under God's mighty hand, that he may lift you up in due time."

Psalm 34:18 (NIV) - "The Lord is close to the brokenhearted and saves those who are crushed in spirit."

These verses reinforce the importance of humility, surrender to the Lord, and the potential for restoration and transformation when one acknowledges one's weaknesses and seeks God's guidance in the process of change and recovery.

5.2 The challenges of helping a narcissist acknowledge and address their behavior.

Just like an alcoholic struggles with returning to his bottle, a narcissist may relapse into their behavior. Recognizing and addressing narcissistic behavior can be an uphill battle, filled with challenges and obstacles. The same principles of recovery that apply to substance addiction can be used by a narcissist seeking to acknowledge and address their behavior. However, the journey can be complex and require significant patience and understanding from those offering assistance.

One challenge in helping narcissists acknowledge and address their behavior is their deep-rooted need for control and dominance. Narcissists are driven by an inflated sense of self-importance and a constant desire for admiration and attention. Consequently, they may be resistant to seeking help or admitting that they have a problem. Breaking through this barrier requires finding a delicate balance between offering support and maintaining firm boundaries while allowing them to maintain a sense of control over their journey.

Another challenge lies in the narcissist's tendency to deflect blame onto others. They often have difficulty taking responsibility for their actions and may instead shift blame onto those around them. Engaging in constructive conversations and addressing the core issues can make it extremely challenging. It is crucial to approach these discussions with empathy and compassion while gently guiding the narcissist to take ownership of their behavior.

The inherent grandiosity of narcissists can also hinder their ability to acknowledge their behavior. They believe they are superior to others and are therefore inclined to dismiss any criticisms or concerns raised about their actions. Helping them see the reality of their behavior may involve presenting concrete evidence and examples, highlighting its adverse impacts on their relationships and personal well-being.

The constant need for validation and admiration can become a hurdle in the change process. Narcissists often seek fulfillment from external sources, relying on the approval and attention of others to bolster their self-esteem. This dependency on external validation makes it difficult for them to recognize and address their shortcomings.

Philippians 2:3-4 (NIV) - "Do nothing out of selfish ambition or vain conceit. Rather, in humility value others above yourselves, not looking to your own interests but each of you to the interests of the others."

Galatians 6:1 (NIV) - "Brothers and sisters, if someone is caught in a sin, you who live by the Spirit should restore that person gently. But watch yourselves, or you also may be tempted."

These verses emphasize the importance of humility, compassion, and gentleness when helping someone acknowledge and address their behavior. It's a reminder to approach the situation with a heart that values others and seeks their well-being, even when dealing with challenges like narcissism.

Galatians 6:1 (NIV) tells us, 'Brothers and sisters if someone is caught in a sin, you who live by the Spirit should restore that person gently. But watch yourselves, or you also may be tempted.' We must be careful not to be tempted by the sins of others. We must be wise when helping those who have fallen into sin. We should be gentle and show compassion but also mindful of ourselves and our temptations. We all have weaknesses, and we must be aware of them when helping others. We should not put ourselves in a situation where we are vulnerable to temptation. We should be careful not to get too involved with the person we are trying to help and make sure to set boundaries. We should also try to understand them and their circumstances and treat them with kindness and respect. We should offer advice and support but not be forceful or judgmental. We should strive to be a good example for them and give them guidance and support. This way, we can help them restore themselves and move past their sin.

It is essential to assist narcissists in developing a healthier sense of self-worth, one that is not reliant on the admiration of others.

It is imperative to remember that the journey of self-awareness and change cannot be forced upon a narcissist. They must be willing and motivated to acknowledge their behavior and work towards change. Patience and persistence are necessary virtues in this process. Encouraging them to seek therapy or counseling can provide a safe place to explore their behavior and make meaningful strides toward personal growth.

Helping narcissists acknowledge and address their behavior can be challenging and complex. By understanding the same principles of recovery that apply to other forms of addiction, such as substance abuse, we can navigate the difficulties of supporting a narcissist through their journey of self-awareness. Establishing boundaries, addressing their tendency to deflect blame, and assisting them in building a healthier sense of self-worth are all important steps in this process. Ultimately, change must come from within, and offering patience, empathy, and support can create an environment conducive to their personal growth.

5.3 Guidance on supporting a narcissist through therapy or counseling.

Counseling can only help if the person is honest and transparent during counseling. It is crucial for individuals seeking support to be willing to open up and share their feelings, thoughts, and experiences with their therapist or Pastor. Like any other individual, narcissists must recognize the importance of being genuine and truthful to make progress. Trust and honesty form the foundation for growth and healing in therapy.

Alongside honesty, another important factor to consider is faith. Faith is essential for narcissists to believe they can change and stay committed to the therapeutic process. This faith can be likened to the Bible's story of Peter walking on water. In Matthew 14:22-32, Peter's faith allowed him to defy gravity and walk on water momentarily. But he began to sink when he doubted and allowed fear to infiltrate his thoughts. This story serves as a reminder that unwavering faith in the Lord and the therapeutic process is crucial for personal transformation.

Hebrews 11:1 (NIV) - "Now faith is confidence in what we hope for and assurance about what we do not see."

Supporting a narcissist through therapy or counseling requires patience and understanding. As a helper, it is crucial to encourage them to find faith in God and their ability to change and to stay the course. Remind them of moments in their lives when they have overcome challenges through faith and determination. By fostering a sense of hope and empowering their belief in their ability to change, you can motivate them to persevere through the difficulties that arise during counseling.

Providing them with biblical verses and stories that emphasize the importance of faith and perseverance is helpful. Sharing stories like the perseverance of Job in the bible or the transformation of Saul to Paul can serve as inspiration for the narcissist in therapy.

Supporting a narcissist through counseling entails being a source of unwavering support and encouragement. Encourage them to embrace vulnerability, as being transparent and open is essential for growth. Remind them that change is a journey that requires time and dedication. By fostering faith, faith that they can change, and in the Lord's ability to change them, and determination to stay and complete their counseling, people who endure and persevere in counseling come out changed; people who quit when it gets complicated and contentious don't. You can help them navigate the challenges and inspire them to achieve personal growth and transformation.

CHAPTER SIX

THE DIVINE CONNECTION: NURTURING YOUR RELATIONSHIP WITH GOD (JAMES 4:10)

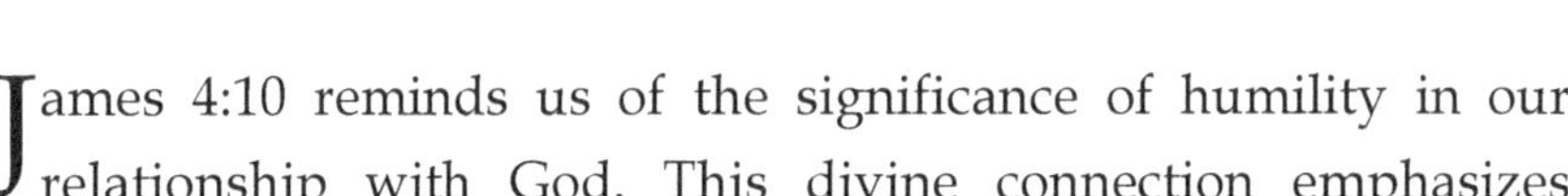

James 4:10 reminds us of the significance of humility in our relationship with God. This divine connection emphasizes vulnerability as a pathway to authentic connections, including our connection with the Lord.

James 4:10, "Humble yourselves before the Lord, and he will lift you up." (James 4:10, NIV)

Embracing Humility:

Humility is a cornerstone of any authentic connection, and our relationship with God is no exception. It involves acknowledging our limitations, imperfections, and our need for divine guidance and grace. Humility is not about talking humbly or trying to look humble; that's pride. Humility is about exposing your true self and your heart's content despite the fear of being exposed and judged. It is a willingness to be vulnerable and accept and surrender to the Lord's will. It is a willingness to serve others and accept their shortcomings. It is a recognition of our imperfections and limitations. It is an appreciation of the gifts and talents of others. It is a recognition of the truth that we are all created equal. It is a recognition that we should be thankful for what we have and what we have been given. Humility is essential to have a healthy relationship with others and to live a life of joy and fulfillment. To be humble is to be humble before the Lord and to have a heart that is open to Him.

Vulnerability in Prayer:

Vulnerability in prayer is an act of humility. It is an invitation to God to come and pour out His grace and mercy on our lives. When we open ourselves to Him, we surrender ourselves, allowing Him to fill us up and speak into our lives. We are asking Him to come into our lives to help us with our struggles and to minister to our hearts. When we are vulnerable in prayer, we recognize our dependence on Him and that He is the only one who can truly make a difference in our lives. It means sharing our deepest thoughts, fears, and desires with Him, recognizing that He knows all things and is able to provide us with the help, comfort, and direction we need. We can trust Him completely when we come to Him in prayer, and we can be sure that He will answer in the best way possible. Being vulnerable in prayer is a sign of our faith in Him and our desire to please Him and receive His grace. It is a powerful way to demonstrate our love for Him and to invite Him into our lives. Prayers take a lot of effort and time, but they are worth it. Prayers that are prayed from a powerful, genuine, and righteous place are mighty prayers. These prayers are powerful because they have a purpose and they are sincere. They are genuine because they come from the heart, not just from the mind. They are righteous because they are in line with God's will. Praying mighty prayers shows that you truly believe in the power of prayer and the power of God. It is not just words but also actions that you are taking. Mighty prayers can alter the course of events, change the hearts of people, and bring miraculous answers to difficult situations. When you pray with faith and an open heart, you can expect to see God's intervention in your life and in the lives of others. Pray with faith and confidence that God will answer you and do just what you ask. Pray mighty prayers and watch God move in your life and in the lives of those around you.

Letting Go of Self-Centeredness:

Nurturing our relationship with God requires letting go of self-centeredness, a trait often associated with narcissism. James 4:10 encourages surrendering our pride and ego to the Lord's will. Self-centeredness is celebrated in the world, but it grieves God's heart because it robes the believer of the resurrection life that comes from dying to self. Self-centeredness also robs the believer of the joy that comes when they focus on giving and serving others. It fosters selfish ambition and pride that can be destructive to relationships and can prevent someone from experiencing the love and joy of God. Letting go of self-centeredness means making God, service to others, and eternal things the motivating force in your life. It means looking past the material things and influences that the world offers - money, people, things, influence - and instead seeking to make a difference in the lives of those around you. When we free ourselves from our selfish desires, we can turn our focus to what truly matters - living a life of true purpose and meaning. This means refocusing our thoughts and energies in accordance with God's will and not our own. It means being willing to take risks, to be vulnerable, and to trust God and those around us. It means being open to change and growth and being willing to surrender our own desires in order to serve a higher purpose. When we do this, we no longer fear the world around us but instead embrace its challenges and use them as opportunities for growth. When the world has lost its grip on us, the devil has nothing left to use to cause us anxiety or depression. We have stolen his weapons and replaced them with a life of purpose and meaning that is rooted in God and His love.

Finding Strength in Surrender:

It is in our surrender to God's will that we find strength. Transparency becomes a source of empowerment as we trust in His wisdom and love to guide our lives. Surrendering to the Lord means surrendering our will to His will and submitting to His authority. Taking up our cross means to follow Jesus' example and take up our cross and follow Him. Lifting our hands in surrender means acknowledging that our lives are in God's hands and trusting Him.

The Divine Response:

James 4:10 also assures us of God's response to our humility. When we are an open book, he promises to lift us, providing comfort, guidance, and spiritual growth as we journey together. To be an open book before the Lord means to be honest and transparent with Him about your thoughts, feelings, and struggles. It means to come before Him with an open heart and ready to receive His guidance and direction. It means being willing to listen to what He has to say and obedient to His commands. It means to be willing to share your burdens with Him and to trust Him to carry them.

A Transformative Journey:

Nurturing our relationship with God is a transformative journey that requires ongoing humility and vulnerability. It calls us to seek His presence and guidance in all aspects of our lives. A transformative journey is a journey that requires us to be constantly open to change and growth. We must examine our hearts and be willing to allow God to work in our lives to transform us. It is a journey of spiritual transformation that requires self-reflection and a desire to grow closer to God. Jesus said in Revelation 3:20, 'Behold, I stand at the door and knock. If anyone hears my voice and opens the door, I will come into him and eat with him, and he with me.' When we are transparent before the Lord, it means that our hearts and minds are open to Him. If we have an open door, the Lord will bless us with his presence and grace. Open your heart to the Lord today, and don't delay. Invite the Lord into your life, and you will experience an abundance of joy and peace. When we make ourselves open and available to the Lord, He will fill our lives with purpose and hope. Let go of worry and fear, and be open to the Lord's plan for your life. Don't be afraid to open the door and let Him in. The blessings and joy that will follow are worth the effort.

6.1 Prayer and Meditating on the Word for Transformation

Prayer and meditation on the Word offer inward and upward journeys, fostering sanctification, humility, and a deeper connection with the Lord.

As an act of vulnerability, prayer enables individuals to engage in a soulful conversation with the Lord. It involves acknowledging one's weaknesses, seeking the Lord's guidance, expressing gratitude, and surrendering one's desires and fears. Through prayer, a direct and intimate connection with God is established, fostering a sense of authenticity and trust in the relationship with the divine.

"Do not be anxious about anything, but in every situation, by prayer and petition, with thanksgiving, present your requests to God." (Philippians 4:6, NIV)

Meditating in the Word brings sanctification and introspection; it allows the Word to take root, move in, and start renovating. This self-awareness helps uncover and address narcissistic tendencies as individuals gain deeper insights into their behaviors and attitudes. The number one reason I believe people do not change is because they do not think or see that they have a problem.

"Search me, God, and know my heart; test me and know my anxious thoughts." (Psalm 139:23, NIV)

Both prayer and meditation on the word have the potential to nurture empathy within the believer. Through these practices, individuals gain a deeper understanding of their experiences, emotions, and character, so they are better equipped to empathize with others. This enhanced capacity for empathy is crucial in overcoming narcissism, as it fosters a more compassionate and understanding approach towards others.

The Bible tells us in Ephesians 4:32, NIV, "Be kind and compassionate to one another, forgiving each other, just as in Christ God forgave you." Ephesians 4:32, NIV

Regular prayer and meditation on the word will often lead to inner peace. This will take us into the Spirit's presence, where anxiety is no more; individuals can confront their narcissistic tendencies with patience and self-compassion from this place of rest and find restoration. These spiritual disciplines offer opportunities to seek the Lord's guidance and wisdom and allow God's word and opportunity to renovate the heart, creating a receptive heart and a deeper connection with the Lord.

"Be still, and know that I am God; I will be exalted among the nations, I will be exalted in the earth." (Psalm 46:10, NIV)

Consistency in prayer and meditating on the word cultivate personal growth, resilience, and humility. Over time, these practices instill a sense of connection with both God and brothers and sisters in the Lord.

6.2 Surrendering to God's Will

Surrendering to God's will is the ultimate act of vulnerability. It involves letting go of our desires, ego, and self-centered tendencies to align our lives with God's divine plan. This act of submission is transformative and has an impact on overcoming narcissism.

Embracing God's plan is at the core of surrender. It means acknowledging that His plan is more significant and wiser than ours. It requires us to trust that His guidance will lead us on the path of righteousness as we allow the Lord to take control. Narcissism often stems from the desire for control and self-centeredness. Surrendering involves relinquishing this need for control and allowing God to take the reins of our lives.

It brings inner peace. Surrender alleviates the burdens of self-absorption and allows us to find solace in the knowledge that God controls our lives. It brings peace and tranquility amid the storms of life and there uncertainties.

Vulnerability and trust are crucial aspects of surrender. It requires us to place our trust in God completely. This vulnerability involves believing that His intentions are ultimately for our good and that He knows what is best for us. This leads to a more authentic and purposeful existence, free from the trappings of narcissism. Surrender becomes a lifelong journey involving continual self-reflection, sanctification, humility, and a willingness to yield to God's guidance through his word in every aspect of our lives.

6.3 Growing Spiritually through Vulnerability

Growing spiritually through vulnerability is a life-changing journey; it is a path that encourages individuals to open their hearts, embrace righteousness, and deepen their connection with God.

Vulnerability becomes the catalyst for personal and spiritual growth. It involves acknowledging one's imperfections, weaknesses, and the need for divine guidance. As individuals open their hearts to God's presence, they become more attuned to His guidance and wisdom.

One of the key aspects of growing spiritually through vulnerability is developing a humble and contrite heart. This humility allows us to release our ego-driven desires and self-centered tendencies. It creates a space for God's grace to flow, transforming hearts and minds. Psalm 51:17, ESV says, "The sacrifices of God are a broken spirit; a broken and contrite heart, O God, you will not despise."

To be broken before the Lord is to humble oneself and acknowledge one's need for God. It is to recognize that without Him, one is lost and without hope. It is to acknowledge that our strength and wisdom are not enough and seek the Lord and His guidance in our lives. To be broken before the Lord is to lay down our pride and self-sufficiency and to trust in Him for our salvation and ultimate victory. It is to lay down our worries and fears and to give them all to Him. It is to surrender our hearts and minds to Him, trusting Him to bring us out of our brokenness and to lead us in the paths of righteousness. To be broken before the Lord is to come to Him in repentance, acknowledging our need for His forgiveness and grace. It is to recognize that in Him we find healing and hope and that we are made whole in His presence. To be broken before the Lord is to place our trust in Him and to seek His guidance in all things. It is to find comfort in His presence and to know that, no matter what, He will never leave us nor forsake us.

Vulnerability in prayer and meditating on words is crucial in this growth process. It allows us to lay bare our fears, doubts, and insecurities before God. In these vulnerable moments, they discover God's unconditional love and acceptance.

We develop a deeper sense of empathy and compassion as we grow spiritually through vulnerability. They become more attuned to the struggles and pain of others, leading to a genuine desire to offer support and understanding. "Clothe yourselves with compassion, kindness, humility, gentleness, and patience." (Colossians 3:12, NIV)

A sense of inner peace and contentment marks this spiritual growth journey. It arises from the realization that true fulfillment comes from aligning our lives with biblical principles rather than pursuing self-serving ambitions.

6.4 Embracing the Transformation through Selflessness (Galatians 2:20)

Embracing transformation through selflessness is a powerful theme focused on vulnerability. Galatians 2:20 serves as a guiding light in this transformative journey, reminding us of the impact of selflessness on our spiritual growth.

"I have been crucified with Christ, and I no longer live, but Christ lives in me. The life I now live in the body, I live by faith in the Son of God, who loved me and gave himself for me." (Galatians 2:20, NIV)

This scripture underscores the notion that true transformation begins when we surrender our self-centered desires and allow Christ to live in and through us. It involves a radical shift from self-absorption to selflessness, where our actions and intentions are guided by love and a genuine concern for others.

In the journey of embracing transformation through selflessness, humility becomes our constant companion. It involves recognizing our limitations and imperfections, acknowledging that we are not the center of the universe, and extending compassion to others. "Do nothing out of selfish ambition or vain conceit. Rather, in humility, value others above yourselves." (Philippians 2:3, NIV)

This transformation is marked by a willingness to sacrificially serve and give of ourselves to meet the needs of others. It involves actively seeking ways to positively impact the lives of those around us, embodying the selflessness exemplified by Christ.

"For even the Son of Man did not come to be served, but to serve, and to give his life as a ransom for many." (Mark 10:45, NIV)

Embracing transformation through selflessness is not a one-time event but a lifelong commitment. It requires daily self-examination and a genuine desire to grow in love and empathy. As we align our lives with the selfless love of Christ, we become vessels of His grace, impacting the world around us in meaningful ways.

CHAPTER SEVEN

HEALING AND EMBRACING A NEW CHAPTER: MOVING ON FROM NARCISSISM

The journey of healing and moving on from narcissism is a process that demands patience, self-compassion, and spiritual guidance. Just as in the biblical narrative of redemption and restoration, individuals seeking to break free from the shackles of narcissism can find hope in the promise of healing and transformation.

Embracing Forgiveness for Self and Others

Healing begins with forgiveness, both for oneself and others. Ephesians 4:32 (NIV) encourages us to "Be kind and compassionate to one another, forgiving each other, just as in Christ God forgave you." In the context of narcissism, forgiveness is a powerful act of liberation. It involves letting go of resentment and recognizing that we are all imperfect.

Forgiving oneself for past narcissistic behaviors is an essential step toward healing. It allows individuals to break free from the chains of guilt and self-condemnation. Similarly, extending forgiveness to those whose selfish actions may have hurt you is an act of healing for both parties. This process may be challenging, but it is crucial to moving forward.

Cultivating Self-Compassion and Self-Worth

Moving on from narcissism entails cultivating self-compassion and rebuilding self-worth. Instead of seeking validation from external sources, individuals must learn to find their value from the Lord. Recognizing our intrinsic worth as God's creation is a powerful antidote to the insecurities bred by narcissism.

From the dawn of time, humans have sought validation from external sources. Narcissism, a form of vanity, has been an ever-present temptation, leading individuals to place too much value on their appearance or worldly possessions. But Psalm 139:14 (NIV) reminds us that our worth is not found in these things because "we are fearfully and wonderfully made" by the Lord. Knowing that we are loved and valued by our Creator is the only way to find true security in our identity.

Rather than relying on the approval of others, we must learn to find our value in God's unconditional love and grace. We can no longer allow ourselves to be held captive to the whims of the world. Instead, we must strive to find our security within our relationship with the Lord. We must choose to believe that we are indeed "fearfully and wonderfully made" in His image and that our worth lies in His hands.

Only when we come to this understanding can we break free from the chains of narcissism and insecurity. We can begin to find peace and joy in the knowledge of our true value as God's beloved creation. We can be secure in being loved and accepted by our Creator and find our worth in Him alone. This is the only way to truly find peace and security in our identity.

Self-compassion involves treating oneself with the same kindness and understanding we would offer a friend. It means acknowledging our imperfections without judgment and embracing our humanity. Galatians 5:22-23 (NIV) speaks of the fruits of the Spirit, including "gentleness and self-control." These qualities guide us toward self-compassion and emotional healing.

Seeking Professional Support and Guidance

Healing from narcissism often requires professional support. Just as individuals needing physical healing consult physicians, those on a journey of emotional healing should seek therapists or counselors. Proverbs 11:14 (NIV) reminds us of the wisdom in seeking guidance: "For lack of guidance, a nation falls, but victory is won through many advisers."

Therapists can provide valuable insights, coping strategies, and a safe place for individuals to explore their emotions and behavior patterns. This therapeutic journey helps individuals gain self-awareness, develop healthier relationships, and work through the underlying issues contributing to narcissism.

Rebuilding Authentic Relationships

Moving on from narcissism involves reevaluating and reconstructing relationships. Authentic connections are founded on vulnerability, empathy, and mutual respect. Romans 12:10 (NIV) encourages us to "Be devoted to one another in love. Honor one another above yourselves." In the context of narcissism recovery, this means valuing others' needs and feelings.

Rebuilding relationships may require making amends for past actions and demonstrating a commitment to change. It also involves setting boundaries and being accountable for one's behavior. By nurturing authentic connections, individuals can experience the support and acceptance necessary for their healing journey.

Embracing a New Chapter

Narcissists who have broken free from their narcissism often feel condemnation and frustration, but it is important to remember that Christ died so that your sin can be forgiven. It is not an easy journey, but if you stay the course, eventually, the people you have hurt will only remember the now, the love you are showing them now, the care you are showing them now, and the love you are giving unconditionally. It won't be easy, but it is possible to look back and move forward without being weighed down by regret and guilt. As you start to take steps towards healing, focus on the hope that comes with the knowledge that Christ died for you and your sin can be forgiven and washed away. Put your trust in Him and allow yourself to take those steps forward. By doing this, you will soon be able to look forward to a brighter future full of love and care for yourself and others.

7.1 Provide encouragement and support for individuals in relationships with narcissists.

Like any sin, compassion and empathy for those grappling with narcissism remain crucial. Concerning individuals who have endured relationships with narcissists, it is paramount to view them as victims who have undergone significant suffering. Acknowledging the pain they have endured is the initial step in providing them with the encouragement and support required for their healing and progression.

Narcissistic relationships can inflict enduring wounds upon the individuals involved. Often, these individuals become trapped in a web of manipulation, gaslighting, and emotional abuse. Grasping the depth of their suffering remains indispensable in delivering appropriate support. Compassion empowers us to extend comfort and affirmation to these victims, assuring them that their experiences are validated and their emotions are genuine.

Empathy is pivotal in connecting with individuals who have grappled with narcissists in relationships. We can better understand the emotional turmoil they have weathered by placing ourselves in their shoes. Empathy enables us to identify and acknowledge their sentiments and provide the support they require. Through this acknowledgment, we can establish a bedrock of trust and understanding, prerequisites for their healing journey.

It is crucial to remember that the person involved in a relationship with a narcissist is the victim, and they warrant such treatment. Frequently, these victims experience isolation and bewilderment and may even blame themselves for the abusive behavior they have encountered. Offering encouragement necessitates reminding them that they are not alone, that the abuse was not their fault, and that a brighter future is attainable.

Assisting those who have endured relationships with narcissists can manifest in various forms. Creating a secure environment where they can openly share their experiences and express their feelings without judgment is vital. This can be facilitated through one-on-one dialogues, support group participation, or therapy sessions. Additionally, equipping them with resources such as books, articles, or podcasts on narcissistic abuse can empower them to educate themselves and gain better insights into their circumstances.

Ultimately, the encouragement and support extended to individuals who have weathered relationships with narcissists can significantly contribute to their healing and personal growth. By approaching them with compassion and empathy, acknowledging their suffering, and providing a nonjudgmental listening ear, we can play a pivotal role in their path to recovery. Together, we can aid them in reclaiming their lives and fostering healthier, more fulfilling relationships in the future.

7.2 Advice on rebuilding self-esteem and regaining emotional stability.

Rebuilding self-esteem and regaining emotional stability are crucial steps to healing from the aftermath of a narcissistic relationship. These relationships often leave individuals feeling emotionally depleted and questioning their self-worth. Here is advice on how to rebuild self-esteem and regain emotional stability:

- **Self-Reflection:** Start by taking time for self-reflection. Understand that the narcissist's behavior or opinions do not determine your worth. Reflect on your positive qualities, strengths, and accomplishments. Make a list of your achievements, no matter how small they may seem.

- **Self-Compassion:** Practice self-compassion and self-kindness. Treat yourself with the same kindness and understanding that you would offer a friend facing a similar situation. Be patient with yourself as you heal.

- **Set Realistic Goals:** Set achievable goals for yourself. Start with small, manageable tasks, and gradually work your way up. No matter how minor, each accomplishment can boost your self-esteem and sense of accomplishment.

- **Seek Professional Help:** Consider working with a therapist or counselor specializing in trauma and self-esteem. They can provide guidance, support, and strategies to help you rebuild your self-esteem and emotional stability.

- **Positive Affirmations:** Practice positive affirmations daily. Replace negative self-talk with affirmations that reinforce your worth and value. For example, "I deserve love and respect" or "I am strong and resilient."

- **Limit Self-Criticism:** Challenge and limit self-critical thoughts. Recognize when you are being overly harsh on yourself and reframe those thoughts in a more balanced and compassionate way.

- **Self-Care:** Prioritize self-care activities that nourish your emotional well-being. Engage in activities that bring you joy, relaxation, and fulfillment. This might include hobbies, exercise, meditation, or spending time with loved ones.

- **Establish Boundaries:** Learn to set and maintain healthy boundaries in your relationships. This empowers you to protect your emotional well-being and treat yourself with respect.

- **Surround Yourself with Support:** Build a support network of friends and loved ones who uplift and support you. Share your feelings and experiences with those you trust, and allow them to be there for you.

- **Forgive Yourself**: Understand that making mistakes or having vulnerabilities is natural. Forgive yourself for any perceived shortcomings or past decisions. Self-forgiveness is an essential part of healing.

- **Focus on Growth:** Embrace personal growth as a lifelong journey. Celebrate your progress, no matter how small, and be open to learning and evolving as an individual.

- **Stay In the Moment:** Stay in the moment, focus on what the Lord is doing in your life today, get involved in outreach, and volunteer at your church. Don't look back; everyone in the bible who did that got into unbelief and spiritual trouble. It's never a good idea. And if you're going to look to the future, do so through the eyes of faith, focus on possibilities, not fearfully. These practices can help reduce anxiety, strengthen your faith, and promote emotional stability.

Rebuilding your life and regaining emotional stability after a narcissistic relationship takes time and effort. It's essential to be patient with yourself and seek the Lord's guidance; at the same time, counselors and Pastors can also be valuable resources when needed. Remember that your worth is intrinsic and not defined by past experiences. By implementing these strategies and investing in your emotional well-being, you can rebuild your confidence and regain emotional stability, setting the stage for healthier and more fulfilling relationships in the future.

7.3 Steps for creating healthier and more fulfilling relationships in the future.

In the context of relationships, Baggage refers to the emotional burdens or unresolved issues that individuals carry from past experiences, particularly from previous relationships. These emotional burdens can significantly impact one's ability to form healthy and fulfilling relationships in the future.

Coming out of relationships with narcissists can often leave individuals with a heavy emotional load. They may have experienced manipulation, gaslighting, emotional abuse, and trauma. These experiences can lead to various emotional challenges, including post-traumatic stress disorder (PTSD), distrust of others, fear of getting hurt again, and heightened sensitivity to criticism.

Victims of Narcissism often experience heightened sensitivity to criticism due to their prolonged exposure to the narcissist's behavior and the resulting psychological trauma. Narcissistic abuse is a form of emotional abuse that can leave victims feeling broken, worthless, and unable to trust in relationships. Victims of Narcissism are often criticized by the narcissist for any perceived missteps, and the steady barrage of negative comments can take a toll on their self-esteem. When victims of Narcissism are on the receiving end of criticism from anyone, they often take it to heart much more than the average person. This heightened sensitivity is an adaptive response to the narcissist's constant barrage of criticism and is a defense mechanism. Victims of Narcissism also may have difficulty distinguishing between constructive criticism and malicious attacks, which can cause them to become highly defensive and have difficulty trusting other people.

Individuals need to address and heal from their emotional baggage to embark on a path of healthier and more fulfilling relationships. Here are some steps to achieve that:

- **Acknowledging and Accepting:** The first step is recognizing that emotional baggage exists and accepting that it can impact your current and future relationships. This acknowledgment is essential for personal growth.

- **Therapy and Counseling:** Consider seeking professional treatment or counseling to work through past trauma and emotional wounds. A trained therapist can provide valuable guidance and support in the healing process.

- **Self-Care:** Prioritize self-care to nurture your emotional well-being. Engage in activities that bring you joy, practice the Lord's presence and self-compassion, and focus on your mental and emotional health.

- **Educate Yourself:** Learn about healthy relationship dynamics and red flags for toxic relationships. Knowledge is empowering and can help you make informed choices in your relationships.

- **Self-Love and Self-Worth:** Build a strong foundation of self-love and self-worth independent of romantic involvement. Develop a sense of identity and confidence that isn't reliant on external validation.

- **Support System:** Seek support from trusted friends, family members, or professionals. A support system can provide guidance, encouragement, and accountability on your journey to healing.

- **Caution in New Relationships:** Approach new relationships cautiously and allow them to develop gradually. Rushing into relationships can sometimes lead to overlooking red flags. Take the time to assess compatibility and ensure that your needs align with your partner's.

By addressing emotional baggage and taking these steps, individuals can increase their chances of forming healthier and more fulfilling relationships based on trust, respect, and mutual fulfillment. It's important to remember that healing is a process that takes time, and seeking support is a sign of strength, not weakness.

CONCLUSION

IT IS CRUCIAL TO UNDERSTAND AND NAVIGATE THE NARCISSIST'S WORLD

Understanding and navigating the world of narcissism is a journey that aligns with God's wisdom in the Bible. John 8:32 reminds us that knowing the truth is the key to freedom. In dealing with narcissists, this truth empowers us to protect our well-being and maintain our inner peace.

To understand the narcissist's world is to gain insight into their manipulative tactics and self-centered mindset. Narcissists often seek admiration and may exploit others for their gain. By recognizing these behaviors, we can shield ourselves from manipulation and resist falling into their snares.

Navigating this world also requires establishing healthy boundaries, practicing assertiveness, and embracing self-care. Just as narcissists may lack boundaries, setting clear limits protects our emotional well-being and prevents them from taking advantage. Being assertive allows us to stand up for ourselves respectfully, refusing to tolerate mistreatment.

Moreover, it's crucial to safeguard our self-esteem and mental health. Narcissists may employ gaslighting to make us doubt our reality and sanity. By understanding these tactics and trusting the Lord, we can withstand gaslighting and maintain a strong sense of self.

Understanding the narcissist's world equips us with the knowledge to make informed choices. Recognizing toxic relationships empowers us to decide whether to continue or disengage from them. This wisdom lets us prioritize our well-being and cultivate healthier, more supportive relationships.

By understanding and navigating the narcissist's world, we protect our hearts, honor our boundaries, and nurture our inner strength. This knowledge guides us towards choices that promote our happiness and spiritual growth.

There is potential for growth and healing for both the narcissist and the individuals affected by their behavior.

In a world marked by narcissism, where self-centeredness and destructive behavior abound, we find solace and hope in the transformative power of Jesus Christ. Just as He mended broken people and performed miraculous deeds, He can heal even the most hardened hearts.

Through the profound wisdom of His word, Jesus brings solace and clarity to the chaotic world of narcissism. The Bible serves as a guide, offering comfort and illuminating our path. It purifies our minds, replacing distorted thoughts with divine wisdom. It reminds us that true healing originates from within and that everyone, including narcissists, has the potential to change.

Romans 12:2 teaches us, "Do not conform to the pattern of this world but be transformed by the renewing of your mind." This verse emphasizes the power of transformation through a renewed mindset. It assures us that, with God's grace, change is possible for all.

Moreover, the Holy Spirit liberates us from the bondage of narcissism. It breaks the chains that bind us to self-centeredness, granting freedom and liberation. Isaiah 61:1 proclaims, "The Spirit of the Sovereign LORD is on me... to proclaim freedom for the captives." These words assure us of Jesus' mission — to bring healing, freedom, and release.

In conclusion, amidst the darkness of narcissism, there is hope. Jesus, the ultimate mender of broken hearts, offers a path to transformation. Through His word, the renewal of our thoughts, and the Holy Spirit's liberation, both narcissists and those affected by their behavior can experience healing and transformation. It is through Jesus' anointing that true change and restoration occur. Let us embrace this hope and trust in His power to mend even the most broken of hearts.

www.ingramcontent.com/pod-product-compliance
Lightning Source LLC
Chambersburg PA
CBHW070844160726
48004CB00001B/493